A Garland Series

The English Stage
Attack and Defense 1577 - 1730

A collection of 90 important works
reprinted in photo-facsimile in 50 volumes

edited by
Arthur Freeman
Boston University

A Treatise

by

John Northbrooke

with a preface
for the Garland Edition by

Arthur Freeman

Garland Publishing, Inc., New York & London

1974

Library of Congress Cataloging in Publication Data

Northbrooke, John, fl. 1568-1579.
  A treatise.

  Reprint of the 1577? ed. published in London.
  Original t. p. reads: Spiritus est vicarius
Christi in terra. A treatise wherein dicing,
dauncing, vaine playes, or enterluds, with other
idle pastimes, &c., commonly used on the Sabboth
day, are reproued by the authoritie of the word
of God and auntient writers ... At London, Imprinted
for H. Bynneman for George Byshop. STC 18670.
    1. Amusements--Moral and religious aspects.
  2. Theater--Moral and religious aspects. 3. Dice.
  4. Dancing--Early works to 1800.

  BV4597.N622   241'.6'5   72-170401
  ISBN 0-8240-0584-8

Printed in the United States of America

Preface

Although Puritan attacks upon the professional and amateur stage, and upon theatre in general, may be isolated from "abuses" texts as early as 1558 (see William Ringler's admirable short account in Stephen Gosson *[Princeton, 1942], pp. 51-82, esp. 51-2 n.), the first wave of concentratedly antitheatrical tract-making begins with John Northbrooke's book, "the first work printed in England in which an attack on the stage was considered of sufficient importance to merit mention on the title page" (Ringler, p. 60).*

Of its author little of any biographical importance is known. He was born in Devonshire at an uncertain date, evidently attended no university, and exercised his otherwise unrecorded ministry in Gloucestershire. From the tone of his writings, as from the choice of his present dedicatee, we may guess him a non-conformist with Puritan leanings. The initial dedication of the Treatise *against stage-plays is dated from "Bristowe," while the epistle "To the Reader" is from Henbury (Glos.). Sir John Yong of Bristol, who is addressed in the former as the "singular good friend" of North-*

PREFACE

brooke, received also the dedication of William Baldwin's Beware of the Cat *(1570, two eds., STC 1244-5), which would certainly suggest Puritan sympathies. Yong died in 1589 (will probate 26 February 1591, PCC 93 Leicester). His wife, "your good Ladie Sarah," is invoked in the Epistle by Northbrooke as well.*

As Northbrooke wrote three books, including the present, each title beginning Spiritus est Vicarius Christi in Terra, *a certain amount of confusion has attended their cataloguing.* STC *[1926] unravels the three correctly, but even the latest* BMC *is so misleading that a short exposition may be useful: the present* Treatise wherein dicing, dauncing, vaine playes or enterluds . . . are Re-proved *was entered on 2 December 1577 to George Bishop, and the undated first edition, STC 18670, is commonly assigned to [?1577]. The British Museum copy, 698.e.26, inexplicably dated in the Catalogue [?1579], lacks C1 as well as a4 (there noted); other copies are at Cambridge, Folger, Huntington, Harvard, and The Library Company of Philadelphia. J. P. Collier edited the text in 1843 (Shakespeare Society) from the 1579 second edition, reset and dated (STC 18671), which, he claimed, "differs in no respect from the earlier undated impression" – but 1579 does corrupt the text slightly without adding or changing anything*

6

PREFACE

material. We have chosen to reprint the W. A. White-Harvard copy of [?1577], collating A^4a^4B-T^4U^2, with the headline of $A3^r$ in a presumably early state, reading wrongly "THE EPISTLE"; in the Huntington copy, also lacking the elusive a4, this is corrected to "DEDICATORIE," but the page is not otherwise reset. Harvard's was purchased by White from Quaritch in 1889 for £8. 8. 0, with an appropriate discount of eight percent.

After 1579 there were no further early editions of this text, British Museum 4403.c.43 et seq. being in fact reprints of The Poore Mans Garden, Northbrooke's most popular work (eight editions between 1571 and 1606, three of them new to the STC-in-progress). Northbrooke's third Spiritus Est is A Breefe and Pithie Summe of the Christian Faith (three editions now known, 1571-1582).

The assault on plays occupies $I1^r$-$L2^v$ in the present edition; in 1579 the same passage begins in $H4^r$. The Theatre and the Curtaine are noticed on $I2^v$, and the unsuitability of even quasi-religious drama ($I4^r$) may especially be remarked. Lowe-Arnott-Robinson 243.

April, 1972   A. F.

Spiritus est vicarius Christi in terra.

A TREATISE

wherein Dicing, Daun‑cing, Vaine playes or Enterluds

with other idle pastimes &c. commonly vsed
on the Sabboth day, are reproued by the
Authoritie of the word of God
and auntient writers.

Made Dialoguewise by Iohn Northbrooke
Minister and Preacher of the
word of God.

Cicero de officijs lib. 1.

We are not to this ende borne, that we should seeme to be created
for play and pastime: but we are rather borne to sagenesse &
to certaine grauer and greater studies.

AT LONDON

Imprinted by H. Bynneman,
for George Byshop.

TO THE RIGHT VVOR-
shipfull, Sir Iohn Yong Knight, his
singular good friend, Iohn Northbrooke
wisheth increase of faith and knowledge in Iesu Christ,
continual health, ioyful prosperity, wyth
as much increase of worship.

Hen I cal to minde (right worshipful) the excel-
lent saying of the diuine Philosopher, that saith, Cicero lib. 1
Non nobis solū nati sumus, ortusque nostri de officijs.
partē patria vendicat, partem parentes, partē
amici. &c. *we be borne not for our selues alone:* 1.Cor.10.24.
but some parte of our birth, our countrey, some
part our parēts, some part our friends do claime,
&c. (Plato did know only, by the light of natural reason, that al ex-
cellente and good giftes came of god, and were giuen to the intente
that a man shoulde therewith helpe and profite others. Of like opinion Iames.1.17.
were all the Philosophers, which had tasted of honest discipline and
learning) made me to enterprise and take this treatise in hand, that I
mought therby helpe those that are diseased with any of these diseases,
either of Diceplaying, Dauncing, or Vain playes or enterludes, which
raigneth tootoomuch by so much amōgst Christiās, (especially in these
dayes and light of the Gospel of Christ &c.) whosoeuer therfore doth
thinke him self to be a member of the commō wealth of Christ, (which
is his mistical body,) he must nedes much more be inforced of Chri-
stian knowledge and charitie, to imploy his labours in bestowing those
giftes which God hath giuen him, to the profit of others, than those
Philosophers, which knew not god aright in his word, through Iesus
Christ.

Saint Paul verie aptly (by a similitude) compareth the churche of 1.Cor.12.12.14.
Christ to a natural bodie. &c. As in the natural bodie euerie mem- 20.
Col.1.18.
ber helpeth the whole: for we see, that there is in a natural bodie such Rom.12.4.5.6.7
an affection and desire of euerie member to helpe and maintaine the o- 1.Cor.12.15.16.17
ther, that not only the senses be readie to do their part and office: as 21.22.27.

A.ij.   the

the eie to see, the eare to heare, the nose to smel, the tong to tast, &c.
& so likewise in the rest of the senses: but also al the other parts of the
bodie do so much care for the whole, that they refuse no danger (though
it be neuer so great) to helpe and succour the same.

1.Cor.12.26.

If anie man then, which beareth the name of a Christian, and of
a Gospeller, shal espy forth anie thing, that may conduce and benefite
the mystical bodie, and doeth not his endeuour to the vttermost to
bring the same ther vnto : verily he is to be thought an vnprofitable
member not worthy (in my iudgemēt) to be accompted of that mēber
of whom Christ Iesus is the head : And also that he had not tasted of
the spirit of god, which neither moued with example of the heathen,
nor with loue towards the brethren, considering the great daungers
that might ensue here vpō, would take some paines, and endeuour to
procure medicines, so farfoth as in him lieth, to ease & help the same.
VVhich (according to my exiled and slender learning) haue made this
little treatise againste Diceplaying, Daunting, and Vaine playes or
Enterludes, giuing herein medicines and remedies against these diseases which most of al trouble the whole mēbers of the body : although
at the first it seeme not toothsome, yet I dare auouch, it is holesome.
VVe can be content (for the health of our bodies) to drinke sharp po-
tions, receiue and indure the operation of extreme purges, to obserue
precise & hard diets, & to bridle our affectiōs & desires &c. much
more shold we so do for the health of our soules. And wher should we
seeke for this helth of our soules, but only at Christ Iesus, who is our
only Phisitiō, who calleth euery one to himself that is burdened & heauy lode and he will refresh thē: this is that fyrie Serpent, that as manie as loke vpon him should liue. this is that Isope which purgeth vs:
this is that red Cow so that blemish not vsed to the yoke, that maketh vs white. This is that Sparrow which was slaine &c. to set vs at
libertie. This is the Lambe that taketh aware our sinnes, original and
actual. This is that Pelicā which giueth out his own hart bloud to re-
main as his yong ones that haue ben stoong to death by the poyson of
Satā. As S. Ambrose saith. Omnia Christus est nobis Si vulnus
curare desideras: medicus est. S' febribus estuas, fons est. Si gra-
uaris inquitate: iusticia est. Si auxilio indiges: virtus est. Si mortē
times: vita est. Si cœlū desideras: via est. Si tenebras fugis: lux est.

Gal.6.1.2.
Col.3.16.
Prouerb.27.23.
Col.1.18.
Ephe.5.23.

Esay.53.4.
Luke.9.17.
Cap.11.28.
Numb.21.9.
Cap.3.16.
2.Cor.6.11.12.

Ambros li 5. de
Virgenibus.

Si tibu quæris:alimentũ eſt. Guſtate igitur et videte quam ſuauis
eſt dominus, beatus vir qui ſperat in eo. *That is: If thou deſire to be
healed (of thy diſeaſe) Chriſt is thy Phiſition: if thou wilt haue awaie
the burning ague (of ſinne) he is thy colde fountaine. If thou be grieued with thine iniquities, he is thy righteouſneſſe: if thou be weake, he
is thy ſtrength: if thou feareſt death, he is thy life: if thou deſireſt heauen, he is the way: if thou wilte auoyde darkneſſe, hee is light: if thou
be hungry, he is thy nouriſhment O taſte therefore and ſee, how ſweete
the Lord is: bleſſed is the man that truſteth in him. After I had gathered togither this ſimple worke (which lay far abroad) & ſo had fini-
ſhed this treatiſe, I muſed with my ſelfe, vnto what Patron I mought
beſt direct the ſame In fine, I found none more fit than your worſhip,
cõſidering your vertuous and godly diſpoſitiõ, which anſwereth your
zelous and true profeſſion of the goſpel (for I am aſſured you vtterlye
deſie and deteſt al kinde of Poperie whatſoeuer) and for that I perceiue
my ſelfe ſomething addict and tyed with the bandes of ſingular &
great friendſhip flowing from you to me, In recõpence wherof (bicauſe
I haue none other treaſures to exhibite vnto you, but onlie this little
talent of my baſe and ſimple learning) I do here dedicate vnto youre
worſhip this booke (named a treatiſe againſt, Diceplaying, Dauncing,
and vain playes on Enterluds) although rude & homely, yet (I doubt
not) plaine & profitable for theſe times of ours wherin we liue: wherin I haue to craue (that nothing more hartily I can obteſt) then your
friendly acceptance of the ſame, for it is a token of my hearty good wil,
remembring the worthy deed of the famous Perſian Prince Artaxer-
xes, ſo much of euerie one commended I humblie obteſt your friend-
lie countenance: and by my ſtrong bulwarke againſt the fuming frea-
tes and belching ires of ſaucie Sicophants, Diceplayers, Dauncers, &
Players, which if you do, I haue my whole deſire, and crõinuallie I wil
poure out prayers vnto the Lord of heauen and earth, to ſende you in
this earthlie manſion continual encreaſe of faith, knowledge and zeale
in the goſpel of Chriſt Ieſu: with proſperitie, and acceſſe of manie bleſſed and happie yeares: with your good Ladie (Sarah.) And after this
life, neuer ceaſſing & endleſſe ioyes in the heauenly Seniorie.*

At Briſtow.

Yours to vſe in the Lord,
Iohn Northbrooke Preacher.

¶ To the Christian and faithful Reader.

Rom.2.17.18.19
28.21.22 24.
1. Timo.5.6.
Gala.2.14.
Iohn.8.42.
2.Timo.35.
Rom.2.28.29.

IF such men, as wil be taken for Chriſtians, would flee & abhorre ſo much the deedes of the Epicures, & Saduces (gentle Reader) as they pretēd to deteſt the name and profeſſion of them, verylye they would refraine, and temper themſelues frō wickedneſſe and miſchiefe, & would vſe and exerciſe vertuous & godly life, no leſſe than they now liue obſtinatly in vice, and behaue themſelues in al their doings both wickedly and vngodly. And again, they wouldenone otherwiſe obſerue, and kepe the commaundements of almighty God, than they now neither feare him, nor dread him at all.

VViſdom.2.3.4
Gene.2.7.
1 Reg.10 4
Pſalm.31.5.
Eccleſi.3.21
Pſal.32.9
Mat.10 28
Luke.23.46
Act.7.59
Reuel.6.9
Mat.5.12
2.Timo. 2.8
VViſdom. 10
Mat.25.41
Rom.1.18
Phil.3.18 19
1.Cor.6.9.10
Reuel.22.15.
Pſal.14.4.8 53.7
2.Pet.3.3.
Iud.1.18
2.Eſdras.1.58
2.Pet.5 10
Iob.14.1
Luke.34
Pſal.39.4
1.Theſ.5.2
VViſd.11.8
Mat.3.2.
VViſd.12.1.2.3
4.5.6.7.
Pſal.90.10
VViſd.11.9 10
2.Pet.1.24
1.Pet.4.7
2.Pet.2.19.20

But vndoubtedly there is not one almoſt, which doth ſo much abhorre the thing it ſelfe in his hart (which thing may plainely appeare by our dayly conuerſation, our maners, and al that euer we do) as we eſchew and flee the name. For how can thoſe men be aſſured in their conſciences, that ſoules are immortal, which for the moſt part liue, as brute beaſtes do? Or that there be rewards repoſed for the godly in heauen, or puniſhment ordeyned for wicked mē in hel, which do in no maner thing feare to trāſgreſſe & breake the cōmaundements of God, and do fal headlong into al kinde of vice and enormities, as though they did imagin, that either god is but a ieſting ſtocke, and a ſayned thing, or the ſoules and bodies do dye both at once? (as Pope Iohn the two & twentith held.)

Now I beſeech thee (gentle Reader) what man is there, whome either the feare of Gods iuſtice doth withdraw from vice and ſin, or yet doth induce and bring in minde to reforme and amende his life? wherin thou mayeſt iuſtly lament, and bewaile the folly & ſtate of men, and much wonder at their blindneſſe, or rather madneſſe, which in ſuch ſhortneſſe & vncertainty of life do ſo behaue themſelues, that they haue no mind of any reformation, or amēdment of our life, when we bee croked for olde age, and haue then ſcarſely one day to liue: far off is it, that we go about, or intēd that thing, when we be yonkers, and in our flouriſhing age. VVhen I remember with my ſelfe, that ſuch is the follie of men, or madneſſe

rather

rather (as I may wel cal it)in deferring the reformatiõ of their life and manners,maketh me forowful. Ecce.5.7 2.Pet.10.&.13 14.

It is a world to fee and to behold the wicked people, how they wreft and turne the names of good things, vnto the names of vices.As if a gentleman haue in him any humble behauiour,thē the Royfters cal fuch a one, by the name of a Loute,a Clinchpoup, or one that knoweth no fafhions:if a man talke godly and wifely,the worldlings deride it,and fay,the yongFox preacheth,beware ycur Geefe,and of a yong faint groweth an old deuil:if a man will not dice,and play,then he is a nigard and a mifer,and no good fellow: if he be no dauncer,he is a foole and a blockhead,&c. If a man be a Royfter,& knoweth how to fight his fight, then he is called by the name of honefty:if he can kil a man,& dare rob vpon the high way,he is called a tall man,and a valiãt man of his hands:if he can Dice,playe,and daunce, hee is named a proper and a fyne nimble man:if he wil loyter and liue idlely vpon other mens labours, & fit al day and night at Cards and Dice,he is named a good companion,and a fhopfellow:if he can fweare and ftare, they fay he hath a ftout courage.If he be a whoremaifter,they fay he is an amorous louer and *Venus* byrde, it is the courfe of youth , he wil leaue it when he is olde.&c.Vpon thefe people wil fal that woe and curfe that Efay the prophet doth pronounce,faying:wo vnto them that fpeake good of euil,and euil of good:which put dronkenneffe for light,and light for dronkénneffe:that put bitter for fwete,& fwete for fowre.Saluft alfo fpeaketh of them faying, *Iampridem equidem vera rerum vocabula amifimus,quia bona aliena largire liberalitas , malarum rerum audatia fortitudo vocatur,* that is to faye, Now of late dayes we haue loft the true names of things,bycaufe the giuing away of other mens goods is called liberalitie,& vnfhame faftneffe in noughtie things,is called high or gentle courage.

2.Pet.2.12

1.Peter.4.3.4

1.Timo.5.13 Ephef.4.28 Eccle 13.16. 17.18 19. Efay.5.11.12.

Efay.5.20

Saluft de coniura= tione catilinaria.

VVhat is a man now a dayes if he know not fafhions, and how to weare his apparel after the beft fafhion?to kepe company,& to become Mummers, & Diceplayers,& to play their twentie,forty or 100.li.at Cards,Dice,&c. Poft,Cente,Gleke,or fuch other games:if he cannot thus do,he is called a myfer, a wretch,a lobbe, a cloune,and one that knoweth no felowfhip nor fafhions,and leffe. honeftie. 1.Pet.4.4.

To the Reader.

To the Reader.

To the Reader.

To the Reader.

Prouer.23.20.21
Cap.28.19.
Eccle.15.11.12.

Iohn.5.25.28.29.
Mat.25.41.46.
2.Pet.3. 10.11.12
1.Thes.5.2.
Cap.4.16.
Mat.25.42.
1.Cor.2.9.
Ca.15.42.43.44
1.Thes.17.

honesty. And by such kinde of playes, many of them are broughte into great miserie and penurye. And there are fyue causes hereof (as I iudge) specially among al the rest.

First is vnbeliefe: for if we supposed not, that those things were fables, which are mentioned in the scriptures euery where of the last day of iudgement, and of the voyce of the Archangell, and of the trump of God, and of the throne of Gods seate, wherat al mē must stand, of the punishment of the wicked, of the euerlasting and blessed life, which the godly after this miserable life shal enioy, of the resurrection of the bodies & soules, eyther to be partakers togither of certaine ioye, or else of certaine paine, and also shall giue his accompt of al things, which he hath done, either intended, by thought, saide, or done, and how he hath vsed gods giftes and creatures, towards his needy members, &c. VVithout al doubt & question they would not liue thus ydlely & naughtily as they do.

Eccleli.5.6.
Ezech.18.321
2.Pet.3.9.
Rom.2.4.

The second cause is, the boldnesse (to sinne) vpon gods mercie: this boldnesse is great in very deede, but yet it is such as they may well ynough deceiue theselues withal. For of boldnesse they haue no sure trial at al. So Salomon saith, say not, the mercie of God is great: he wil forgiue me my manifold sinnes: for mercy and wrath came from him, and his indignation commeth downe vpon sinners. &c. with this boldnesse I say, the wicked enimie of mankinde kepeth man in sinne continually, but like as god graunteth forgiuenesse at the first to the repentaunt: so doeth he also sharply punish those sinners which do continue obstinately (without repentance) in vice and sin. For such men then, as repent not vnfainedly, and purpose to leade newe liues, conceiue a false hope and boldenesse of the mercie of God. And by this meanes that the Diuell setteth forth to men this boldnesse, he bringeth this to passe, that they liue on forth quietly, and securely in vice and wickednesse, and thinke little or nothing with themselues at any time of anye reformation or amendment. And herein they despise the aboundance and riches of the bountifulnesse & long suffering of god, being ignoraunt, that the goodnesse of god doth induce, and lead vnto repentaunce.

The third cause s, the custome of sinne, which is in a manner,

made

To the Reader.

made naturall in long continuance. For like as it is harde for a mã to alter nature: so custome, if it be once rooted , cannot easily bee plucked vp and expelled. And therfore it is that learned men doe cal custome an other nature. It is as a certaine wiseman saith: such vices as we haue accustomed our selues to, from our tender age, cannot be without great difficultie weeded out afterward, whiche thing though it be very certaine and true, yet who seeth not how fondly fathers and mothers bring vp their children in cockering, and pampering them: from their infancie they bee giuen to none other thing, but to pride, delicious fare, and vaine idle pleasures and pastimes.

VVisdo.14.15. Leuit.18.30. Iereme.13.23. Eccli.4.12.12.

Ephe.6.4. Eccle.30.7.9.

VVhat prodigious apparel, what vndecẽt behauiour, what boasting, bragging, quarelling and ietting vp and down, what quaffing, feasting, ryoting, playing, dauncing and dicesing, with other lyke felowship that is among them: it is a wonder to see. And the parents can hereat reioyce and laugh with them, and giue libertye to their children to doe what they liste, neuer endeuouring to tame and salue their wilde appetites. VVhat marueyle is it, if they bee found thus naughtie and vicious , when they come to their full yeares, and mans state , which haue of children bene trayned and entred with suche vice: wherof they wil alwayes taste, as *Horace* saith, *Quod noua testa capit, inueterata sapit.*

Eccl.30.11.12.13.

Horatius.

> The Vessel wil conserue the tast
>   of lycour very long,
> With which it was first seasoned,
>   and thereof smel ful strong:
> Euen so a child, if that he be
>   in tender yeares brought vp
> In Vertues schoole, and nurtred wel,
>   wil smel of Vertues cup.

If these men therfore at any time do fully purpose to repent thẽ and reforme their liuing: as when their conscience moueth them, or the burthen of their sinne pricketh them : yet custome hath so preuailed in them, that they fal into worse and worse enormities, and like mad men desire the reformation of their life.

Eccle.5.7.

Consider

To the Reader.

Confider I pray thee (good Reader) what ioly yonkers and lufty brutes thefe wil be, whē they fhal come to be Citizens, and inter-medlers in matters of the common welth:which by their fathers haue ben thus nicely and wantonly cockered vp: neuer correcting nor chafting them for any faults and offences whatfoeuer. VVhat other thing but this, is the caufe that there be now fo many adul-terers, vnchaft and lewde perfons and ydle Rogues? That we haue fuch plentie of Dicers, Carders, Mummers & Dauncers? And that fuch wickedneffe and filthy liuers are fpred about in euery quar-ter, but only naughty education and bringing vp:wel then, fuche as impute this thing to the newe learning and preaching of the gofpel are fhamefully deceiued, hauing no iudgement to iudge of things No, no, the newe learning and preaching of the Gofpell is not the caufe hereof, but the naughty, wanton and foolifh brin-ging vp of children by their parents, as I haue declared.

Prouerb.13.24.
Cap.23 13.
Ecclefi.7.23.
Cap.30.1.

Alfo the flackneffe and vnreadineffe of the Magiftrates to doe and execute their office, is a great caufe of this:if they that vfe ta-uernes, playing, and walking vp and downe the ftreates, in time of a Sermon:if difobedient children, to their parents : If Dicers Mū-mers; ydellers, dronkerds, fwearers, Rogues & Dauncers, and fuch as haue fpent and made away their liuing in belly cheare and vn-thriftineffe were ftreightly punifhed, furely ther fhuld be leffe oc-cafion giuen to offend, & alfo good men fhould not haue fo great caufe to complain of the maners of men of this Age. Therfore the magiftrate muft remēber his office: For he beareth not his fworde for naught, for he is gods minifter and a father of the coūtrey ap-pointed of god, to punifh offenders: but nowadayes by reafon of libertie without punifhmente, and flackeneffe of men in office, which wink at their faults, caufeth fo many idle players & daūcers to come to the Gallows as there are, for as the wife man faith, who fo prohibiteth not men fo to offend when he may, in a maner cō-maundeth them fo to do : for it is better to be a fubiect to a magi-ftrate vnder whom nothing is lawfull, than vnder him, to whome al things is lawful. I feareme gretly therfore, leaft the heathen mēs feueritie, and ftreightneffe in punifhing vice, fhal be a reproch to our magiftrats, and accufe them at the laft day for their negligence

Luke.14.23.
Deut.21.18 19.
20.21.

Mat.11.20.21.
22 23.4.
Luk.10.12.13.14.

and

and flacknesse herein. It is not inough to punish sinne only, but also to preuent and take away the causes thereof.

The fourth cause is, Securitie in wealth and prosperitie, which *Luke.12.15.* doth inebriate the mindes of men in suche sort, that they neyther remember God, nor constantlye purpose to reforme and amende their liues. Therfore it was wel sayd of one, that like as of prosperitie riot proceedeth: Euen so of riot cometh both other common vices, and also vngodlynesse, and the neglecting of Gods word and commaundements: And as *Seneca* affirmeth, that into great welth and prosperitie, (as it was continual dronkennesse) men fal into a *Seneca.* certaine sweete and pleasaunt sleepe. For as *Publius* saith, Riches, *Publius.* maketh him a foole, whom she cockereth to much. Paul also willeth that warning should be giuen to the rich men, that they waxe *1.Timo.1.* not proude, nor haue their affiance in vncertaine riches, but in the *18.* liuing God, to do good, and be rich in good workes.

This Securitie is verily the mother of al vice, for by the same *1.Thes.5.1.* man is made vnsensible, so that in his consciēce he feeleth not the *Iudges.18.7.10.* anger and wrath of god against sinne : by Securitie mens mindes *2.Pet.2.19.* are brought into a dead sleepe, that they be not pierced one whit with the feare of gods punishment, or with the feare of death, or of the last day, to leaue off their vice and sin. This securitie Christ artificiallye painteth out in Luke, where mention is made of the *Luke.12.16.* rich man, whichwhen his land had enriched, and made him welthy *Ecclesi.11.19.* with a fruitful and plentiful croppe, did not goe about to reforme his liuing, and to repent nor to bestow almes vpon the poore, but studied how to enlarge his barnes, and to make more roome for his corne, and sayd, Now my soule thou hast a great deale layd vp for thee, which wil last thee for many yeares : now therfore take thy rest, eate, drinke and be of good cheare. But in this Securitie, what heard he of god: thou foole, this night thy soule shal be takē away &c. markest thou not, how death cometh sodainly vpō him thinking to haue had al the cōmodities & pleasures of the world, as ease, rest, delicious fare, pastimes, delectations, and safegard of al his goods?

For this cause then, Paule commaundeth vs to awake and bee in a readinesse at al times against the comming of the Lord. Christ

To the Reader.

1.Cor.16.13.
Col.4.2.
1.Thu 5.6.7.8.
1.Pet.4.8.
Mat 25.41.
Cap.24.4 2.43.
44.45.46.48.
49.50.51.
Luke.21.34.35.
Genef.7.5.
Luke.17.26.
27.28.29.
Mat 24.38.
2.Pet.3.20.
Luke 17.30.
1.Cor.10.6.
Wifdo.3.17.18
Iames.4.13.14.

our Sauiour also saith, watch and pray least ye enter into tentatiõ: againe, take heed to your selues, least at any time your heartes bee oppressed with surfeting and dronkennesse, and cares of this life, and least that day come on you at vnwares. For as a snare shall it come onal thē that dwel on the face of the earth, like as it befell and happened in the time of Noe, whē al the world was drowned, and in the time of Lot when Sodome was burned with fire from heauen, so verily the last day shal come sodainely, & at the twinckling of an eye, euen when men loke least for it. These things might be faire examples and sufficient warnings for vs, if wee were not more than senselesse.

The fift cause, is the hope of long life. Among many euilles & naughty affections which folow the nature of man corrupted by sinne, none bringeth greater inconuenience than the inordinate hope of long life, as Cicero saith, no man is so olde and aged, that he perswadeth not himselfe that he may liue a whole yeare. This

Luke.15.2.
Ecclesi.5.7.
Gala.6.7.8.9.10
1.Kingt.10 1.
2.Chro.9.1.
Luke.11.31.32
10.5.5

is the cause why we defer the reformation of our liues, and remēber not, that we haue an account to make at the last day. It is to be wondered, that men do put of, and defer such a great and weightie matter, and loke no more of a thing, which profiteth so much, and is so necessarie vnto saluation. The very heathen I feare me shal in the last iudgement be a reproch to vs Christians, in that we are so slouthfull, and haue almost minde at no time to repent and amend our liuings. *Pythagoras* rule and custome was, whē he wēt

Pythagoras custome.

to take reste, to recken and call to remembraunce what thing so euer he had said or done, good or bad, the day before: which *Virgil*

Virgil.

speaking of a godlye and vertuous man, painteth out to vs learnedly: how he neuer slept til he called to remēbrāce al things that he did that day &c. I can not let passe that which *Seneca* speaketh

Seneca.
Sextus.
Ecclesi.4.25.
Ezra.10.1.
Iob.40.9.
Cap.10.15.
Cap.31.1.
Prouerb.28.13.
1.Cor.11.28.
2.Cor.13.5.
1.Cor.11.31.

of this form and order. *Sextus* (saith he) at the euening ere he wēt to rest, accustomed to aske of his minde certain questions: what ill and naughty condition hast thou this day amended? what vice hast thou withstanded? what art thou better now than when thou didest arise? And after he addeth this: what better forme can there be, than this, to examine the whole day againe in this wise? And this rule saint Paul giueth also, saying, let a man therfore examine
him

To the Reader.

himself &c. if we would iudge our selues, we should not be iudged.

But now of the contrarie, let vs consider our exercises, & how we vse to recken our faultes, and examine the whole day again, at night ere we go to rest and slepe: how are we occupied. verily, we kepe ioly cheare one with an other in banquetting, surfeting and dronkennesse, also we vse al the night long, in ranging from town to town and from house to house with Mummeries and Maskes, Diceplaying, Carding and Dauncing, hauing nothing lesse in our memories than the day of death: for Salomō, byddeth vs remember our end and last day, and thē we shal neuer do amisse: but they reméber it not, therfore they do amisse. The bereuiti of our liue, is compared in Scriptures, vnto the smoke, vapour, grasse, a flower, shadow, a span long, to a weauers web, to a post &c. teaching here by that we should be alwayes preparing to die, for that we know not what hour it wil come: therfore, as wise Virgins let vs prepare oyle readie in our lampes, for doubtlesse the day of the lord is not farre off. Dare we take our rest, and boldely to sleape in these our wicked sinnes, in which if any man should die, (as no man is sure that he shall liue the next morow folowing,) he were vtterly cast away, & condemned body & soule: but alas, these things they reméber not. In such wise they flatter thēselues with hope of longer lyfe, (sith with the which so many men be deceiued how childish are they, or rather how do they dote, which do perswade themselues, that they be exempted out of the number of those, as it were by some singular priuiledge and prerogatiue.

These are the chiefest causes that we liue so wickedly as we do in these dayes. Take away therfore the causes, the effectes wil easily be remedied. And for the curing of three notable vices, (amōg all the reste) I haue here made, (according to my small skill) a Treatise against Diceplaying, Dauncing, and vayne playes or Enterluds, Dialogue wise, betwene Age & Youth, wherin thou shalt finde great profit and commoditie, and how in al ages, times and seasōs, these wicked & detestable vices of ydlenesse, Diceplaying, Dauncing, and vaine Enterludes, hath bin abhorred & detested of al nations, and also among the Heathens, to the great shame & condemnation of Christians, that vse no playe nor pastime, nor

Eccl.7.36.
Iob.7.6.7.9.
Esay.40.6.7.
Psal.3.5.
Ecclesi.14.18.
1.Pet.1.24.
Iames.1.10.
Iob.14.2.
Cap.4.14.
Psal.102.3.11.
Mat.25.4.,
Ephes.5.14.
1.Cor.6.9.10.
Ephes.5.3.,
1.Timo.9.

2.Pet.3.4.
Hebre.9.27.

any

To the Reader.

any exercise more than Diceplaying, Dauncing, and Enterludes: Now therfore (friendly Reader) I haue laboured for thy sake with my poore penne, to bring forth this small volume that thou seest: VVherin I haue to request and desire thy friendly acceptaunce of the same, bycause it is a pledge and token of my good hart & will to thee: for which if thou canst afourde me thy good worde, I aske no more, it shal not be the last (if God lēd me life) that thou shalt receiue of me. As for *Aristarchus* broode, and *Zoilus* generation, lurking loyterers, Dicers, Dauncers, Enterlude Players, & frantike findefaults, dispraysing and condemning euerye good endeuour, I wey them not, I am not the first (though the simplest and rudest,) that their venemous tongs (typped with the Mettal of infamy and slaunder) haue torne in pieces, & vncharitably abused, god forgiue thē. Accept thou therfore, I beseech, the (curteous Reader) this my trauel, & good meaning in the bestpart. Thus I bid thee farewel. From Henbury.

Psal. 12.2.3.4.
Eze. 33.30.31.32.
Psal. 14.6.
Psal. 101.5.
Mat. 5.11.
Act. 7.57.
Iames. 3.8.
Psal. 109.2.3.

Iohn Northbrooke.

¶ An admonition to
the Reader.

Eade this booke with good aduise,
Perpend and wey with diligence,
The counsels graue herein containde,
Then iudge according to the sense:
And so you shal ful soone espie,
The great good wil this authour beares,
To countries wealth, to al mens iey,
To profit youth and old of yeares.
VVherfore do read, and read againe,
Then put in practise what you finde:
So shal you fullie recompence,
In ech respect the authours minde.
And as for scorneful sycophants,
Or Daunters mates what so they say,
He needes not care although they rage,
Let them go packe and trudge away.
These paines he toke for all good men,
For whom he made this little booke,
And for all such as mindeful are,
For Vertues cause therein to looke.
Therfore in fine to God I pray,
That he wil graunt vs of his grace,
Our harts and mindes may ioyne for aye,
Stil to perfist in Vertues trace.

YOVTH.   AGE.

GOD blesse you, and well ouertaken good father Age.

AGE. And you also good sonne *Youth*.

YOVTH. From whence came you nowe good father? if I may be so bolde (to presume of your curtesie) to demaunde of you.

AGE. I came from thence, whereas you oughte to haue bene, and resort vnto.

YOVTH. What place is that, I pray you declare to me?

AGE. In good sooth it is that place whiche you, and suche others as you are, delite very little to come vnto.

YOVTH. I dare holde a ryall, you meane the Church.

AGE. You had wonne your wager if you had layde: it is euen the very same place that I meane.

YOVTH. That place is more fitte for such olde fatherly men as you are, than for such yong men as I am.

AGE. The place is fit, and open for euery man to come and resort vnto, of what estate, condicion, or yeares soeuer he or they be of. *Luc.14.21. 22.*

YOVTH. I graunt that to be true.

AGE, Why then resort you not thither as you ought to do, and frequent it oftener?

YOVTH. I haue great busines other wayes for my profit, in other places, and therefore must doe that first, which is the cause of my slacke and seldome comming to the Church.

AGE. Christe biddeth you seeke first the kingdome of God, and his righteousnesse, and all those things (that you neede of for your bodie) shall bee ministred vnto you. But I perceyue your care is according to the Poetes saying: *O ciues, ciues, quaerenda pecunia primum est, Virtus post nummos*, that is, O Citizens, Citizens, first seeke for mony, and after mony for Vertue. *Math.6.33. Horatius in Epist.*

B.   Take

Take heede therefore, least you be one of that crewe which S.
Augustine exclaimeth againste, saying : *O quam plures sunt ex*
vobis qui prius tabernam visitant, quam templum, prius corpus refi-
ciunt, quàm animam : prius Dæmonem sequuntur, quàm Deum.
O howe many are there of you, which doe first visite the Tauerne, then the Temple, which doe first feede and refreshe their
bodie, then their soule, which doe first followe and wayte after
the deuill, then God. &c. Christe made a scurge of small cordes,
and draue the byers and sellers out of the Temple : but nowe I
see that the Magistrates haue cause to make scurges with great
cordes to driue and compell idle persons, and buyers and sellers
into the Temple.

YOVTH. Cannot I finde Christ aswel in a Tauerne as in a
Temple ? For he sayth : Wheresoeuer two or three be gathered togither in his name, he is in the middes of them.

AGE. Indeede Christe is to be founde in all places, and is
amongst the godly and faithfull gathered togither according to
his will : for his Church and faithfull congregation is not tyed
and bounde to any one speciall place (as the Donatists and Papists affirme) but is dispersed vppon the face of the whole earth
wheresoeuer. I pray you, howe can you say that you are gathered togither in Christes name, when you doe all things to
the disglorie thereof, in breaking of his blessed commaundementes, by your swearings, drunkennesse, violence, violating
the Sabboth daye, neglecting to heare his worde, and to receiue
his sacraments, and to resort to the house of prayer with the godlye congregation. As God is neare to them that call vppon him
in truth, so is he farre from the health of the vngodlye and wicked. Where did Ioseph and Marie finde Christ, when as they
sought after him ? It was in no Tauerne or playing place, but
it was in the Temple, disputing and apposing the Doctors. &c.
To that purpose Saint Augustine sayth : *Quærendus est Chri-*
stus, sed non in platea vbi est magna vanitas : non in foro vbi est
grandis aduersitas : non in taberna, vbi est summa ebrietas : non in
secularia Curia, vbi est maxima falsitas : non in scholis mundano-

Margin notes:
August. ad
fratres in E-
rem. serm. 33
1.Cor.11.21.
Iohn.2.15.
Luc.14.23.
Mat.18.20.
Psal.50.16.
Psal.145.18.
Psal.119.155.
Luc.2.46.
August. ad
fratres in E-
rem. Serm. 43

rum philosophorum, vbi est infinita peruersitas : Chziſt is to bee Ambro.l:b.3. de virg.nib.
ſought foz, but not in the ſtreetes, where is much vanitie : not
in the Iudgement place, where is great trouble : not in the Ta-
uernes where is continuall dzunkenneſſe : not in the wozldly
courtes, where is great decepte : not in the ſchœles of wozldly
Philoſophers, where there is endleſſe contention.

YOVTH. I perceyue that I haue ouerſhotte my ſelfe in
ſaying and doing , as I haue ſayde and done : yet I
pzaye you, gyue mee to vnderſtande, whye you are ſo de-
ſirous to haue hadde mee at Churche eſpeciallye thys moz-
ning ?

AGE. Bicauſe I wiſhe your ſoules health.

YOVTH. Was there a Phiſition at Churche this daye, that Hebr.13.17. 1.Pet.5.2.
coulde miniſter any medicines ?

AGE. Yea that there was, who hath miniſtred ſuch medicines to our ſoules this day, that no tongue can expzeſſe the be-
neſite we haue gotten and obtained thereby.

YOVTH. Was hee a Phiſition foz the bodye, oz foz the
ſoule ?

AGE. You may perceiue by my wozdes, that it was a Phiſition foz the ſoule onely.

YOVTH. So I thought, foz if he had bene foz the bodie, our
Gentlemen and Gentlewomen, with our rich farmours in oure
pariſh, would haue bene there, although they had bene caried in
Wagons oz Coches.

AGE. You haue ſayde truth, and the moze to bee lamented, bicauſe they feele not the diſeaſe of their ſayntie and ſicke
ſoules, noz yet remember the wozdes of Chziſte, that ſayeth :
The whole neede not a Phiſition, but they that are ſicke. Ther- Math.9.12. Heb.13.17. Math.11.28.
foze hee calleth (by his Pzeachers) all thoſe that are wearye,
and laden, to himſelfe, and pzomiſeth to them that come, that
they ſhall finde reſte vnto their ſoules . This Phiſicke is Rom.3.24. Eſa.55.1. Reu.22.17.
gyuen to vs freelye foz nothing, withoute anye oure wozthy-
neſſe, merites, oz deſertes . I woulde to GOD they didde
feele their ſickeneſſe, then they woulde acknowledge it , and Eſay.55.6.
make

make spede to seke for the Phisition whiles he may be found, and

Iohn.6.27. labour for the life which shall neuer decaye nor perishe. I praye

Math.19.23.
Luc.12.21. God the olde Prouerbe be not found true : that Gentlemen and rich men are Uenison in heauen (that is) verye rare and daintie to haue them come thither.

YOVTH. Do you meane all Gentlemen and rich men in generall ?

AGE. No, God forbidde, for I knowe well that there are a

Gal 3 23.
Ac.10.34 35 great number of godly, zealous, & vertuous Gentlemen, Gentlewomen, and rich men, which doe hunger and thirste for the ad-
nauncement and continuall encreasing of Gods glorie and hys

Phil.1.23.
2.Cor.5.12.
Reue.22.20
Rom.4.25, kingdome, to the vtter subuersion of all sinne, wickednesse, vyce, and Poperie, and also doe hunger and thirste to be at home in their euerlasting habitation, prepared for the elect, throughe the death and resurrection of Iesu Christ our only sauiour.

YOVTH. I vnderstande your meaning very well, howe you will vrge and persuade euery man to be a hearer of the sermons.

AGE. You haue sayde the truth, that is my purpose & whole desire, which with all my heart I wishe and pray for.

YOVTH. The Church is no wylde Cat, it will stande still, where as it is, and as for Sermons they are not daintie, but very plentie, and therefore no such great neede or haste to runne to heare Sermons.

AGE. Although they are plentie (God continue it) yet you must not negleʃt to heare Sermons in season and oute of sea-

2.Tim.4.2. son.&c. For it is a speciall argument that Christe our Sauiour vseth to discerne his children from the children of Saten by, whē

Iohn.8.47.
1.Ioh.4.6.
Ioh.10.27. he sayth : he that is of God, heareth Gods worde : ye therefore heare them not, bicause ye are not of God. Againe, My sheepe heare my voice. &c. Saint Gregory sayth: *Certiʃsimum signum est*

Gregorius. *noʃtræ prædeʃtinationis Dei verbum libenter audire,* that is, It is a most sure signe and token of our predestination, gladly and wil-

Luc.10.16.
Mat.10.40
Iohn.13.20 lingly to heare the worde of God. Therefore if you will be of God and of his folde, heare his voyce pronounced to you by his preachers, thereby shall you profite your selfe, please God, and
diʃpleaʃe

displease Satan: Contrarywise you shall displease God, and please Satan, to your owne confusion, which God forbid.

YOVTH. I beseeche you good father, declare to me plainelye by some proofes of holy scripture, that Satan is displeased if wee heare the worde preached or read, and also that he is so well contented when as we neither heare nor reade the worde of God, but continue in ignorance.

AGE. That I will do good sonne (God willing.) You may very well perceyue his nature by that our Sauiour Christ saith: Ye do not vnderstande my talke, bicause ye cannot heare my word: Ye are of your father the deuill, and the lust of your father ye will doe. &c. Also in these wordes of Christ: When the vncleane spirite is gone out of a man, he walketh through drie places, seeking rest, and when he findeth none, he sayth, I will returne vnto my house whence I came out, and when he commeth, he findeth it swepte and garnished, then goeth he and taketh to himselfe seuen other spirites worse than himselfe, and they enter in, and dwell there, so the last ende of that manne is worse than the first. Therfore Saint Peter sayth: your aduersarie the Deuil goeth about like a roaring Lion, seeking whom he may deuour. &c. Saint Paule sayth: If our Gospell be then hid, it is hid to them that are loste, in whome the God of this worlde hath blinded the mindes, that the light of the glorious Gospel of Christ should not shine. &c. Origen sayth: *Dæmonibus est super omnia genera tormentorum, & super omnes pœnas, si quem videant verbo dei operam studys dare, scientiam diuinæ legis, & mysteria Scripturarū intentis perquirentem. In hoc eorum omnis flamma est: in hoc vruntur incendio. Possident enim omnes, qui versantur in ignorantia.* That is, Unto the deuils it is a torment, aboue all kindes of tormentes, and a payne aboue all paines, if they see anye man reading (or hearing the worde of God, and with feruent studie searching the knowledge of Gods lawe, and the mysteries and secretes of the Scriptures. Herein standeth all the flame of the deuils: in thys are they are tormented. For they are seased and possessed of all them that remaine in ignorance. This you haue heard, and may

Io.8.43.44.

Luc.11.24.
Math.12.43:

1.Pet.5.8.

2.Co.4.3.4.

Origen in numer. hō. mil. 27.

easily perceyue that this is he(who by his ministers the Papists) shut vp the kingdome of heauen before men. This is that serpent that beguileth vs, that our mindes shoulde be corrupte from the simplicitie that is in Christ, he can transforme himselfe into an Angell of light. This is he that soweth Darnell amongst the Lords wheate. This is that ennimie that commeth and taketh away the word of God out of our hearts, least we should beleue, and so be saued.

Math.23.13
2.Cor.11.3.

Math.13.3.
Luc.8.12.
Mar.4.2.

YOVTH. What meaneth this latter sentence that you recited, I pray you declare it to me.

AGE. Christ hereby manifesteth what is the propertie and nature of Satan, how he can abide no mã for to heare the word of God, and obey it, knowing wel that faith cõmeth by hearing, & hearing by the word of God, and that they cannot heare but by the preaching, &c. therefore he practiseth by all wayes and meanes to make vs deafe, that we may not heare the preaching, and so beleue, and be saued . Therefore my sonne marke this well, that when as you, or such others, doe little delite, or lesse regard to heare Gods worde preached, that Satan doth possesse you and them, and is become your maister, and you his seruauntes and bondmen, as Paule sayth : Knowe ye not, that to whome soeuer you giue your selues as seruants to obey, his seruants ye are to whome ye obey, whether it be of sinne vnto death, or of obedience vnto righteousnesse. Thus you see what an ennimie Satan is to mans saluation, and his wages that he giueth, is eternall death.

Rom.10.17.

2.Tim.2.26

Rom.6.16.
Ioh.8.34.
1.Pet.2.19.

Reue.12.10
Rom.6.23.

YOVTH. Howe many wayes doth Satan go about to hinder vs from hearing the worde of God ?

AGE. He doth this by sundry meanes and wayes.

YOVTH. I pray you declare thẽ to me as briefly as you may.

AGE. I will so. First he doth it by corruptiõ of our natures, and also by reason we are accustomed continually to sinne. Secondly by a vaine hope and trust in our selues and our freewill. Thirdly by an Epicurial and worldly care. Fourthly, by encouraging our selues to doe wickedly, by the examples of other men that

that daily offende. Fiftlye, by pleasures, pastimes, and such like. Sixtly, by his owne craftinesse and subtiltie. Seuenthly, by tearing vp slanders vpon the preachers of the worde of God. Eightlye, by open persecution. &c. These are the wayes and practises that commonly he vseth.

YOVTH. I assure you they are dangerous practises and easie meanes to drawe vs from hearing the worde of God. Yet hitherto you haue not expressed to me whether there be any daunger or punishmente threatened against suche as will not heare Gods worde?

AGE. I was about so to doe, if you had not interrupted mee in my talke so soone.

YOVTH: I pray you let me heare them, that by those threats I may learne to auoyde the daunger that may ensue vpon me in not hearing the Sermons.

AGE. As the curses are great against the contemners and negligent hearers of Gods worde, so the blessings are double fold to the diligent and obedient hearer, accorging to that saying in Logique, *Contraria inter se opposita, magis elucescunt,* that is, Contraries being set one against the other, appeare more euident, so by the curses, you may the better consider of the blessings.

Deut. 28. 13.
Deut. 28. 1.
Leuit. 26. 3.

YOVTH. In deede I shall so, therefore speake on, I beseech you.

AGE. It is written in Deuteronomie: If thou wilt not obey the voice of the Lord thy God, all these curses shall come vpon thee, & ouertake thee. Cursed shalt thou be in the town, & cursed in the field, cursed is thy basket & store, cursed shall be the fruit of thy bodie, and the fruite of thy lande, the encrease of thy kyne, and the flockes of thy sheepe. Cursed shalte thou be when thou commest in, and cursed when thou goest out. The Lorde shall sende vpon thee, cursing, trouble, and shame, in all that whiche thou settest thyne hande to doe, vntill thou bee destroyed, and perishe quicklye. The Lorde shall make the Pestilence cleaue vnto thee, vntill hee hathe consumed thee from the lande, the Lorde shall smyte thee wyth a Consumption,

Deut. 28. 15.
16. 17. 18.
19. 20. 21.
22.
Lamē. 2. 17.
Leui. 26. 14.
Baruc. 1. 20.

and

and with the feuer, and with a burning ague, and with feruent
heate, and with the fworde, and with blafting, and with mel-
dew. &c. as in that Chapter you maye reade throughly, wherein
you fhal finde moft terrible plagues vpon thofe that are contemners and difobeyers of God and his worde. In Samuell you
may reade alfo that Saule was reproued for this fault, and lofte
his kingdome for it. Hath the Lorde (faith Samuell) as greate
plefure in burnt offrings and facrifices, as when the voyce of the
Lorde is obeyed? Behold to obey is better than facrifices, and to
harken is better than the fat of Rammes: Bicaufe thou haft caft
away the worde of God, therefore he hath caft away thee from
being king. Salomon fayth, bicaufe I haue called and yee refufed, I haue ftretched out my hande, and none woulde regarde,
but ye haue defpifed all my counfels, and wold none of my cor-
rection. I will laugh at your deftruction, and mocke when feare
commeth. Then fhall they call vpon mee, but I will not aun-
fwere, they fhall feeke me earely, but they fhall not finde me, bicaufe they hated knowlcdge, and did not chofe the feare of the
Lorde, they woulde none of my counfell. Therefore fhall they
eate the fruite of their owne way, and be filled with their owne
deuifes. Againe he fayth: He that turneth awaye his eare from
hearing the law, euen his praier fhal be abhominable. Reade Ieremie, and fee what plagues came vpon the people for their neglecting of Gods worde. Ezechiell fayth, that a booke was deliuered him (againft thofe that contemned and woulde not heare
the worde of the Lorde, and frame their liues aunfwerable to it)
which was writté within and without, Lamentations, & mour-
nings and wo. They that were called to the fupper, and refufed
to come, had pronoũced againft them, that none of them which
were bidden, fhall tafte of his fupper. He fayeth alfo, that the
kingdome of God fhall be taken from you, and fhall be giuen to
a nation which fhall bring fruites thereof. Alfo you may perceiue
by Chriftes weeping ouer Ierufalem, when hee prophecied of
their deftruction, for not comming to him when he called, and for
killing his Prophetes who were fent to call them to repentance:

howe

Margin notes:
1. Sam. 15. 22
Ierem. 7. 23
Prou. 1. 24.
25. 26.
Prou. 28. 9.
Iere. 44. 23.
Ezech. 2. 10
Cap. 33. 31.
32. 33.
Luc. 14. 24.
Mat. 21. 43.
Luc. 19. 41.

how wrathfull Gods indignation is against all suche. &c. Uerye well did Saint Paul saye: See that ye dispise not him that speaketh : for if they escaped not whiche refused him, that spake on earth, much more shal wee not escape, if wee turne away from him, that speaketh from heauen. &c. Chrisostome sayeth : *Quanto namq́, maior gratia, tanto amplior postea peccantibus pœna.* The greter benefites we receiue (at Gods h̄ndes) and doe abuse them, or not regard them, the greater punishment shall fall vpon them afterward.

Hebr.12.25

Chrisost.ad populum Antioch. komil.21.

YOVTH. These sayings out of the Scriptures are terrible, and pearce my hart and conscience very deepely.

AGE. You knowe that the worde of God is a two edged sworde, and entreth through (sayeth Saint Paule) euen to the deuiding asunder of the soule and the spirite, and of the ioyntes, and the marie, and is a discerner of the thoughtes and ententes of the heart. Whereby you see that it woundeth mortally the rebellious: but in the electe it killeth the olde man, that they should liue vnto God.

Heb:4.12.

YOVTH. These paines and curses are terrible, which maketh me to trimble for feare.

AGE. Si horrescimùs pœnam, horrescamus etiam causam pœna: If we do abhorre and feare the punishment, let vs also abhorre and feare the cause of punishment (which is sinne.)

Lauaterus in Paralip.ca.3

YOVTH. I perceiue now that it is a greate sinne, and they are in a great danger that contéptuously refuse to heare the word of God when it is preached.

AGE. It is most true. For as Augustine sayeth : *Non minor erit reus qui verbum dei negligenter audierit, quàm ille qui corpus Christi indignè sumit,* That is : Hee is no lesse guiltie that negligently heareth the worde of God, than he that eateth vnworthily the body of Christ. Saint Cyrill sayeth : If we doubt of them that heare the worde preached, what shal we do of them that doe neuer heare the word preached at all?

August.1. causa 1.quest cap.interrog

1.Cor.11.29

Cyril in Leui. lib.6.

YOVTH. Wil not ignoraunce excuse vs?

AGE. Nothing lesse, for it will rather accuse vs, as Augustine

C3

Augustin Epist.105.

stine sayth : *Ignorantia in eis qui intelligere noluerunt, sine dubita-tione peccatum est, in eis autem qui non potuerunt, pæna peccati. Er-go in vtriusq̄e non est iusta excusatio, sed iusta damnatio.* Igno-raunce in them that woulde not vnderstand, without doubt it is sinne : in them that coulde not vnderstande, it is the punishment of sinne. For in eyther of them there is no iuste excusation, but

Conc.Toleta 4.can.24.

iuste damnation. Therefore was it called the mother (not of de-uotion, as the Papistes tearme it) but of all mischiefe and vice. But wee maye saye of our aduersaries the Papistes, as Irenius

Iren.lib.2. Cap.9.

sayde against the Valentinian heretikes. *Veritatis ignorantiam, cognitio iem vocant,* Ignoraunce of the truth, and blindnesse, they call knowledge.

  YOVTH. There are a number that perswade with themsel-ues cleane contrary, & thinke no offence lesse, nay, that it is no of-fence at all, to absente themselues from the Sermons, and neuer scarce come to the Temple at prayer, hauing no iuste (but rather vniust) occasions to followe their owne pleasures in whatsoeuer, and yet boldely wil say and affirme (as I my selfe haue heard thē) they are Gospellers and Protestants, and doe beleeue very well in God, and knowe as muche as the Preacher can, or is able to say or teach them.

Mat.7.21.

  AGE. Christ sayth : Not euery one that sayth Lord, Lord, shall enter into his kingdome, nor euerye one that can saye the Lords prayer, the beliefe, and the ten commaundements, is a good Protestant, but they that do the will of our heauenly father. So the Iewes bragged that they had Abraham to their father, and

Iohn.8.41.

that they were not borne of fornication, but that they hadde one father whiche is God : yet Christe pronounceth, that they are of their father the Deuil, for his workes they did. And amongst all the workes, Christe speaketh of this sinnefull worke of Satan, which was, their bragging that they were Gods children, and yet

Psal.50.17.

woulde not heare Gods worde. But to those shall be sayde : What art thou that takest my couenaunt in my mouth, and hatest to be reformed, and dost cast my words behind thee? &c. Although these

Mat.17.5.

meane can saye well, yet (for that they shewe not obedience to

t, the

their heauenlye father, that sayeth : This is my onely begotten sonne, heare him.) he wil distroy them with the hypocrites, that professe they knowe God, but by workes they deny him, and are abhominable and disobedient, and vnto euery good worke reprobate (as Saint Paule saith.) Hillarie speaketh of these men, saying : *Multi sunt qui simulantes fidem, non subditi sunt fidei, sibiq; fidem ipsi potius constituunt quàm accipiunt,* that is : There are many that counterfayte fayth, and yet they are not subiect or obedient to the (true) faith : these men do rather prescribe to them selues a fayth, than to receiue (true) faith and religion.

Rom.1.21.
Titus.1.16.

Hila.lib.8.de trinitate.

YOVTH. They say that they belieue wel, and haue the true faith notwithstanding.

AGE. Hearke I pray you, what Saint Cyprian sayeth to them, *Quomodo dicit, se credere in Christum, qui non facit quod Christus facere præcepit?* How can he say, that he belieueth in Christe, that doth not that which Christ hath commaunded? Whereby you may see howe wide these people are from true religion. It was wel sayde of Saint Augustine, *Constat fidem stultam non solum minimè prodesse, sed etiam obesse,* It is certaine that a foolishe fayth not onely doth no good, but also hurteth. Therefore (if you and they repent not) yee shall one daye feele the iust reward therof : when in your tormentes and endlesse paynes yee shall be forced, wyth the wicked in hell, to crye and saye : Wee haue erred from the way of truthe, and haue wearied our selues in the waye of wickednesse and destruction. And we haue gone through daungerous wayes, but the way of the Lord wee haue not knowne. What hath pryde done to vs? or what profite hath the pompe of riches brought vs?

Ciprian de simplicitate prælatorum.

August in quæst ex vet. Testamenti quæst.45.

2.Thess.1.8.

Psalm.75.8.
Wisd.5.6.

YOVTH. I praye you, what causes are there to moue and perswade vs, that wee oughte to heare and reade Gods holye word?

AGE. There are foure principal causes.

YOVTH. What are they?

AGE. The first cause (to moue vs to heare & read the word of God) is, the commandement of almightie God our heauenly father,

Deut.30.4.

Handwritten at top: *Note reaſon for hearing Word*

father, which ſayeth : Ye ſhall walke after the Lorde your God and feare him, and ſhall kepe him commaundements, and hearken vnto his voyce. Againe, the Lord thy God will rayſe vp vnto thee a Prophete like vnto me, from among you, euen of thy brethren, vnto him ſhalt thou hearken. &c. Thys is my welbeloued ſonne, heare him. &c. He that heareth you, heareth me, and he that diſpiſeth you, diſpiſeth me, &c. The Scribes and Phariſies ſit in Moyſes ſcate, al therfore whatſoeuer they bid you obſerue, that obſerue and doe. &c. If ye loue me, keepe my commaundements, &c. Search the Scriptures, for in them ye thinke to haue eternall life, and they are they which teſtifye of me. &c.

The ſecond cauſe is, the ende that we were created and redeemed for, that is, to learne to knowe God, to honour him, worſhippe him glorify him, to feare him, loue him, and obey him, as our God and father, as Chriſoſtome ſayeth : *Omnia condita eſſe propter hominem, hunc autem conditum eſſe propter deum, hoc eſt ad agnoſcendum & glorificandum deum. &c:* All things were ordayned to be made for man, man was ordeyned to be made for God, to the end to knowe and glorifie God. &c. So Dauid ſaid: I ſhall not die but liue, and declare the workes of the Lorde. So Paule ſayeth: Glorify God in your bodie and in your ſpirite, for they are Gods. Againe: Whatſoeuer ye doe, do all to the glorie of God.

The thirde cauſe is our owne infirmities, for that we are nothing, we knowe nothing, nor can perceyue any thing, as of our ſelues, without the helpe of Gods ſpirit, and the word of his promiſe. Ireneus ſayth : *Cùm impoſſibile eſſet ſine deo diſcere deum, per verbum docet Deus homines ſcire Deum :* When it was impoſſible to knowe God without God, God by his worde teacheth men to knowe God. So Dauid ſayeth: that a yong man ſhall redreſſe his waye, by ruling himſelfe accoding to Gods word. His worde is a lanterne to our feete, and a light to our paths. &c. The law of the Lord is perfect, conuerting the ſoule, the teſtimonie of the Lord is ſure, and giueth wiſedome vnto the ſimple : the commaundements are pure, & giue light vnto the eyes: by the

Marginal references:
Deut.30.2.
Deut.18.15.
Math.17.5.
Math.3.17.
Luke.10.16
Mat.10.40
Iohn.13.20.
Mat.23.23.
Iohn.14.15.
Iohn 5.39.
Act.17.11.

Malac.1.6
Chr.ſoſt.

Pſal.118.17.
Pſal.86.12.
1.Cor.6.20
2.Theſ.3.12
1.Cor.10.30

2.Cor.3.5.

Ireneus.

Pſal.119.9.
105.
Pſalm.19.7.

Rom.15.4.

15

is thy seruant made circumspect, and in keeping of them there is great rewarde. Saint Paule sayeth : What soeuer things are written afore time, are writtē for our learning, that we through pacience, and comforte of the Scriptures might haue hope. I gaine : The whole Scripture is giuen by inspiration of God, and is profitable to teach, to improue, to correct, and to instructe in righteousnesse, that the men of God maye be absolute, beeing made perfect vnto all good workes. That is, sayeth *Bruno*, it is profitable to teach them that are ignoraunt to reproue and conuince them that speake against the faith : to correcte sinners : to instruct those that are rude and simple. Chrisostome also sayeth: *Quicquid quaritur ad salutem: totum iam impletum est in Scripturii, qui ignarus est, inueniet ibi quod discat, qui contumax est & peccator, inueniet futuri iudicij flagella qua timeat, qui laborat, inueniet ibi glorias & premissiones vita aterna:* Whatsoeuer is sought for saluation, is wholy conteyned & fulfilled in ý Scriptures, he that is ignorant, shal finde ther what he ought to learne, he that is a stubborn and disobedient sinner, shal finde there scourges of the iudgement to come, which shall make him feare, he that laboureth and is oppressed, shall finde there promises and glory of eternal life.

The fourth and last cause is, the sharpe punishment that god pronounceth againste suchr, as you haue hearde declared before, when we talked of Gods curses and plagues. Christ sayth himself, this is ý condemnation, that light is come into the worlde, and men loued darknesse rather than light, ticause theyr deedes were euill. &c. Thus you haue hearde the causes why we ought to heare Sermons preached by those that preach Christ truly, & to read the holy Scriptures.

YOVTH. These causes are excellent, & of great importance, and of necessitie to be considered of al men.

AGE. You say truely, they are so, yet for your better instruction, I pray you answere me to these questions which I shall demaunde of you.

YOVTH. I wil if I be able.

AGE.

2.Tim.3.15

2.Tim.3 16
Prima in.2.

Chrisost in
Math.22.
homil.41.

Deot 28.15.
16.17.18.

Iohn 3 19.

A G E. Why doth God erect his throne amongst vs?

Y O V T H. Bycause we should feare him.

A G E. Why doth he reueale his will vnto vs?

Y O V T H. Bycause we should obey him.

A G E. Why doth he giue vs his light?

Y O V T H. Bycause we should see to walke in his wayes.

A G E. Why doth he deliuer vs out of troubles?

Y O V T H. Bicause we should be witnesses that he is gracious.

A G E. Why doth he giue vs his worde?

Y O V T H. Bicause we should heare learne, and know him.

A G E Why doth he call vs by his Preachers?

Y O V T H. Bicause we should repent and so come to him.

A G E. Why doth he giue vs his sacramentes?

Y O V T H. Bicause they are seales of his promise, that we shuld not be forgetfull of the benefites purchased for vs by the precious body and bloud of our sauiour Iesus Christ.

A G E. Why doth God giue vs vnderstanding?

Y O V T H. Bycause we should acknowledge him.

A G E. Why doth he giue vs a will?

Y O V T H. Bycause we should loue him.

A G E. Why doth he giue vs bodies?

Y O V T H. Bicause we should serue him.

A G E. Why doth he giue vs eares?

Y O V T H. Bicause we should heare him.

A G E. You haue answered truely and directly, wherby I per-
Luc. 12. 47
ceiue you haue read the Scriptures, and haue some knowledge of Gods wil: and therfore sith you knowe your maisters wil, and doe it not, you shal be beaten with many stripes.

Y O V T H. Is it sufficient then to heare the word of God preached, and so to be hearers only?

Iames. 1. 21.
22.
23.
24.
A G E. No. For as you ought to heare, so must you be a do-
er thereof. Saint Iames sayeth: Receyue with meekenesse the
worde that is graffed in you, whiche is able to saue your soules.
And be ye doers of the worde, and not hearers onlye, deceyuyng
your owne selues. For if any heare the worde, and do it not, he is
lyke

like vnto a manne, that beholdeth his naturall face in a glasse. For when he hath considered himselfe, he goeth his waye, and forgetteth immediatly what manner of one he was. &c. Saint Paule also sayeth: The hearers of the Lawe are not righteous before God, but the doers of the Lawe. Wee are (sayeth hee) hys workemanshippe created in Christe Iesu vnto good workes which god hath ordeyned, that we should walke in them. Herein (sayeth Christ) is my father glorifyed, that wee beare muche fruite. Whosoeuer heareth of me these wordes, and doeth the same, I will liken him to a wise builder. &c. Christ ioyneth hearing and doing togither, with a true Copulatiue, saying: *Beati qui audiunt sermonem dei & obseruant eum:* Blessed are they that heare the word of God, and keepe it. Therefore Christ biddeth our light (that is, our faith and religion) to shyne to the worlde, that the world may see our good workes, and glorifye our heauenly father. &c. Wherby we may see, that wee ought, and must needes haue, wyth hearing, doing: with faith, workes: wyth doctrine, lyfe: with knowledge practise: with science, zeale: with professing, expressing: with hearing, keeping: with wordes, deedes: with talking, walking. So that these muste needes dwell togither in one house, as Mary and Martha, two sisters, whiche ought to bee *tanquam Comites indiuidui:* he that hath my commaundements, sayth Christe, and keepeth them, is hee that loueth mee. &c. Sainte Augustine vppon these wordes, sayeth: *Qui habet in memoria, & seruat in vita: qui habet in sermonibus, & seruat in moribus: qui habet in audiendo, & seruat in faciendo, aut qui habet in faciendo, & seruat in perseuerando, ipse est qui diligit me,* Hee that hath (my worde) in hys memorie, and keepeth it in life: hee that hath it in wordes, and keepeth it in manners: he that hath it in hearing, and kepeth it in doing: or he that hath it in doing, and keepeth it in perseuering and continuing, he it is that loueth mee. You see then, that wee must not onelye be hearers, but also doers of the word. It shall not bee asked (at the dreadfull daye of Iudgemente) howe muche we haue heard or readde, or howe much we do know, but

how

Rom.2.13.

Ephes.2.10

Iohn.15.8.

Mat.7.24.

Luc.11.28.
Math.5.16.
1.Pet.2.12.
Iames.2.26.

Luc.10.59.

Iohn.14.21.

August.in Iob.tract.75

Gene.14.13
Math.25.35.

2.Cor.5 10.
Iames.2.18.

August in
Psal. 66.

Luke.8 8.
Math.13.2.
Mark.4.8.
Titus.1.15.

Heb.6.8.
Mat.25 .41

Mat.3.10

how wel we haue liued. What workes we haue expressed, to testifye with vs of our spiritual regeneration & inward fayth. &c.

S. Augustine sayth: *Audire veritatem nihil est si non auditionem fructus sequatur,* To heare ye truth is nothing, vnlesse there follow fruites of our hearing. Therefore we must be that good grounde wherin the seede of Gods word is sowen, which bringeth fruite an hundreth, sixtie, and thirtie folde. For we ought not to be like those that professe they knowe God, and denie him with theyr workes. That ground that bringeth forth such thornes and briers, is neare vnto cursing, whose ende is to be burned. For euery tree that bringeth not forth good fruite, is hewen downe and cast into the fire.

YOVTH. I perceiue now that the doctrine of the Gospell is not a Libertine doctrine, to giue a carnall libertie to men, to do and liue as they liste, or that all workes, fasting, prayers, and almes deedes, obedience, &c. are ouerthrowen or denyed thereby, as the Popes Catholikes haue and do report.

Rom.3.31.

AGE. By this doctrine of the Gospell, as you heare, is established and confirmed al godly life, and good workes. But thys hath bene alwayes the practises of Satan and his Impes, falsely to report of this doctrine, as we reade in the holye Scriptures.

YOVTH You haue satisfied me in this point (I thanke god for you) yet I pray you giue me to vnderstand what he was that preached this day at our Church?

AGE. I assure you I know not his name, but whatsoeuer his name be, he is a godly learned man, one that beateth downe mightily by the word of God. al Popish religion and superstition, and therewith he is a great enemy to sinne and vice whiche nowe raigneth to to much amongst al estates and degrees, and a great friend to vertue and true religion.

Act.9.22.
2.Cor.10 4.
Rom.3.10.

2.Cor.1.17.
1.8.19.
2.Tim.3 14
Exod.28.30

YOVTH. I am very glad to heare so good a report of him as I do, it is glorious when the Preachers are certaine of their doctrine which they teache, constant therin, and leade liues answerable thereto, hauing that *Vrim* and *Thummim* whiche sygnifieth

Aeth knowledge, and holynesse, declaring thereby what vertues are required in those that are Ministers and Preachers of Gods worde and sacraments, so as they may builde vp Gods Church, both with doctrine and conuersation of lyfe. *1. Tim.4.12* *2. Tim.3.10* *1.Cor.9.27*

A G E. God defende but that they shoulde be such, as in all respectes they may shewe themselues to the worlde, an ensample in worde, in conuersation, in loue, in spirite, in fayth, and in purenesse, and that they shewe themselues lanternes of light, and ensample of good workes, with vncorrupt doctrine, with grauitie and integritie.&c. *1. Tim.4.12* *Math.5.14.* *Titus.2.7.*

Y O V T H. Your greate commendation of this Sermon maketh mee sorrowfull that I had not bene at it, but my businesse was such as by no meanes I could be there.

A G E. Was your businesse so great, that it might not haue bene deferred and put off for that present, vnto another time? I pray you, may I be so bolde as to vnderstande of you, what this great businesse was, that thus hindered you from hearing so notable and worthie a Sermon as was preached this morning?

Y O V T H. I may shewe you, for anye great weyght that it was of. But whatsoeuer it was, I put you out of doubt, it was about no matters of any common wealth.

A G E. Then belike you were at prayer with all your familie, in your owne house.

Y O V T H. I tell you truth, I prayed not, but I haue playde all this night, that this morning I coulde scarce holde open my eyes for sleepe, and therefore was fayne for to recouer my losse sleepe this forenoone.

A G E. You haue herein abused Gods ordinaunce, and your selfe also. For God made the daye for man to trauell in, and the night for man to rest in.&c. *Psa.104.10* *23.* *Psal.74.16* *Psa.136.8.9*

Y O V T H. Why good father, is it not reason that a man shuld take his rest, and sleepe when he pleaseth.

A G E. Yes in dede, so that he vseth his rest and sleepe moderately and orderly, that he may the better go about those lawfull affayres that he hath to doe. For otherwise (as you vse your rest

D. and

Prou.20.13
and sleepe) shall happen to you, as Salomon sayth: He that loueth sleepe shall come vnto pouertie. &c. Our life is a watching,

Mark.13.35
1.Peter.5.8.
therefore we ought to take heede, that wee lose not the greatest part of our life with sleepe, namely, sith of the same many vices be engendred as well of the bodie as of the mynde. Cato to thys effect sayth:

Plus vigila semper, nec somno deditus esto,
Nam diuturna quies vitijs alimenta ministrat.

YOVTH. You knowe that sleepe was giuen for mans preseruation, for that nothing hauing lyfe is there that sleepeth not. Aristotle sayeth, that all creatures hauing bloude, take their repose

Arist.lib.4.
de anima.
and sleepe. &c. Sleepe is a surceasing of all the senses from trauel, which is, or is caused by certaine euaporations and fumes ryfing of our meate and sustenance receyued, mounting from the stomacke immediately vnto the braine, by whose great coldenesse these vapors warme are tempered, casting into a slumber euery the forces or senses exterior, at which time the vitall spirites retiring to the heart, leaue all the members of the bodie in a sleepe, vntill such time againe, as these sayde vitall spirites recouer new force and strength to them againe, and so these vapors, or ceasing, or diminishing, man agayne awaketh, and returneth to himselfe, more apt to his businesse, than at any time before. And therefore to sleepe and take muche rest, is not so noysome or hurtfull as you affirme.

AGE. You haue herein shewed your selfe like a Philosopher and a Phisition: but farre wyde eyther from good Philosophie or wholesome Phisicke. Although it be good and necessarie for the bodie, yet must it not be with excesse, and immoderately taken:

Arist.
for that to much sleepe sayth Aristotle, weakeneth the spirites of the bodie, as well, as also of the soule, euen as moderate and competent rest bettereth them, increasing their vigor and their force, euen so immoderate rest hurteth and weakeneth. For as manye things are necessarie and needefull in mans lyfe, so taking in excesse and out of season, annoy and grieue much: as to eate, who feeleth not howe hunger vs compelleth, and yet he that eateth too much,

much, repenteth it, as we commonly see. Sleepe then must bee taken, for necessitie onely, to reuiue, refreshe, and comforte the wearye senses, the spirites vitall, and other wearye members. For too much sleepe (besides that it maketh heauie the spirits and senses, the partie also becommeth slouthfull, weake, and effeminate with ouermuche ydlenesse) ingendreth much humiditie and rawe humors in the bodie, which commonlye assaulte it with sundrie infirmities, messengers of death, and of finall ruine. For when we sleepe too muche, all the moystures and humors of the bodie, with the naturall heate, retire to the extreme parts therof, no where purging or euacuating whatsoeuer is redundant. So then vnmeasurable sleepe is not onely forbidden by Philosophers and Phisitions but also is a thing odious to the wise. Ouid with other Poetes, terme sleepe an Image, or pourtraite of death, saying:

Ouid.

> VVhat else thou foole, is sluggishe sleepe,
>   but forme of frosen death?
> By setled houres of certaine rest,
>   approch thy want of breath.

Therefore be you (and all suche as you are) ashamed then, that spende the greater parte of your tyme in ydlenesse and sleepe in your beddes, vntill you bee readye to goe to youre dynner, neglecting thereby all dutie of seruice both towardes God and man. These are the men that one speaketh of, saying: *Diu dormiunt de mane, & sero cito cubant de nocte,* They will go verye late to bedde at night, and sleepe long in the morning. Surelye he that so doth, his offence is nothing lesse than his, that all daye doth sitte in fatte dishes, surfetting lyke a grosse and swollen Epicure, considering these creatures shoulde onely bee taken, to the sole sustentation and maintenance of life, and not to fill or pamper voluptuouslye the bellye. Dionysius sayeth: *Non viuas, vt edas: sed edas vt viuere posses: ad sanitatem, non ad incontinentiam habenda est ratio,* Thou lyuest not to eate, butte: eate as thou mayest lyue: For there

Holcot in lib Sap.cap.4.

Dionys. in Rom.cap.13.

must

must be a gouernement to vse it for thy health, and not to incontinencie. Chrisostome sayth : *Non vita est propter cibum & potum, sed propter vitam cibus & potus.* The life is not appoynted for meate and drinke, but meate and drinke is appoynted for the life. In which sort we must take our sleepe, onely for necessitie, and nothing for ydle pleasure, and that in due time, and not out of season, that we may the better serue God and our neyghbours. If that yong man Eutichus, for sleeping at Paules sermon at Troas in a windowe, fell downe (as a punishment of God) from the thirde lofte, deade, what punishment then thinke you, will God bring vpon you and other like, that sleepe from the sermon ? and neuer come to diuine seruice, but sleepe oute Sermons and all, which commeth to passe by your night watchings and ydle pastimes, therefore no excuse will serue you herein.

YOVTH. Why good father, is not this a lawfull excuse for me to be absent from the Temple, at prayer and preaching ?

A G E. It is no more lawfull excuse for you, than it was for them, that were called to the supper, which seemed to make lawfuller and more honest excuses than you do : when as one would go to his ferme, another to proue his Oxen, and another to abide with his newe maried wife, &c. All which things of themselues, and by themselues, are good and lawfull. But when these things are occasions to hinder vs, and drawe vs backe from our obedience vnto oure G O D in his worde, then are they turned into sinnes, as Salomon sayth : He that turneth away his eare from hearing the lawe, euen his prayer shall be abhominable. The reason is, bicause it is not of faith, which fayth is grounded vpon Gods worde. For whatsoeuer is not of faith, is sinne. For where a true fayth is, there is alwayes obedience to Gods worde, for faith hath hir certaintie of the worde of God, and true obedience wayteth vppon fayth continually, as one of hir handmaydes.

Therefore, if lawfull things (of themselues) as Oxen, Fermes, wyues, children, setting our houshold in order, burying of our fathers, prayers, sacrifices, good intents & meanings, our own

liues,

Chrysost. in
Gene.cap.6.
homil.23.

Act.20.9.

Luc.14.20.

Mat.10.37.
Luc.14.26.
Eccl 39.26.
Eccl.39.27
Proue.28.9

Rom.10.17.
Rom.14.23

Psal.122.

Luc.14.16.
Mat.10.37
Ierem.7.23

liues,&c.are not to be preferred before Gods calling,o2 can be any
excuse to vs at all: Howe muche lesse shall our vayne and ydle
playes and wanton pastimes, be an excuse vnto vs at the dreadfull day of iudgement, though they can say (as Salomon repor-
teth of them) Come let vs enioy the pleasures that are present,let
vs chearefully vse the creatures as in youth, let vs fill our selues
with wine and oyntments, and let not the floure of life passe by
vs: Let vs be partakers of our wantonnesse, let vs leaue some
token of our pleasure in euery place: for that is our portion and
our lot: Yet in the ende they shall be forced to say in bitternesse of
heart (if they repent not) we haue wearied our selues in the waye
of wickednesse and destruction, but the way of the Lord we haue
not known: what hath pride and pleasures of our youth profited
vs.&c. Horrible is the ende, sayeth Salomon, of the wicked generation.&c.

YOVTH. All this I must needes confesse to be true that you
haue sayde: yet as Salomon sayth,there is a time for all things,
a time to play, a time to worke, a time to builde, a tyme to pull
downe.&c.

AGE. If you confesse my saying to be true, and yet doe
contrarie, you shall be beaten with manye stripes. For as Saint
Iames sayth: To him that knoweth howe to doe well,and doth
it not, to him it is sinne. This he spake to such as sayde in hys
time, as you doe nowe, that confessed what was good, but they
woulde not doe it. And as for this place of Ecclesiastes or Preacher, by you alleaged,to maintaine your ydle sportes and vayne
pastimes, is not well applied by you. For he speaketh of this diuersitie of time, for two causes. First, to declare, that there is nothing in this worlde perpetuall, *Omne creatum finitum est*, All
things created be finite, that is, it hath and shall haue an ende.
So Seneca sayth: *Nihil est diuturnum, in quo est aliquid extre-*
mum. Secondly, to teach vs to be pacient, and not grieued,if we
haue not all things at once,according to our desires, neyther enioy them so long as we woulde wish,and not therby to maintaine
ydlenesse and vayne pastimes. So may the Drunkerde, Adulte-

Math.8.22.
1 Sam.15.23
2.Cr.26.17
1.Cro.13.10

VVis.2.6.
Isa.22.13.
1.Cor.15.32.

VVisd.5.7.

8

VVisd.2.19.

Eccle.3.1.2.
3.4.5.6.7.

Luc.12. 47
Iames.4.17.

1.Iohn.2.17
Marc.13.32.
2.Pet.3.11.12
1.Cor.7.31.
Esay.40.8.
Luc 12.18.
Genes.6.13.

Senec.lib.2

Iam.5.7.

rer, Vsurer, Thiefe, &c. (with the whole rabble of wicked and vngodly ones) likewise, and to the same effect and purpose alledge this place, and applye it for their practises, as you doe for yours. But Syrach teacheth you another lesson, saying : God hath commaunded no man to doe vngodly, neyther doth he giue any man licence and time to sinne. &c. This doth well appeare by the wordes of Saint Paule, saying : Whyle we haue time, let vs doe good. &c. Saint Ambrose vpon these wordes, sayth : *Tempus enim idcirco conceditur vita, vt iam iustè versemur,* that is : Time is therefore graunted vnto our lyfe, that wee shoulde lyue rightly and iustly all the dayes of our life. The godlye man hath alwayes sayde : *Veritas filia temporis est, & mater omnium virtutum,* that is : Truth is the daughter of time, and the mother all vertues. And that no time nor houre ought to be spent ydelly, appeareth by that Christe himselfe sayde : The Kingdome of heauen is lyke vnto a certayne housholder that wente to hire labourers into his vineyarde, hee went the third, the sixt, the ninth, and the eleuenth houre, founde some standing ydle, and sayde to them, why stande ye here all daye ydle ? Goe yee also into my vineyarde. &c. Whereby it appeareth that wee oughte to waste and spende no time, nay, no houre in ydlenesse, but in some good exercise. &c. as it maye onelye redounde to the glorie of the immortall name of God, and profite of our neyghboures. Verye well was it sayde of one, vpon these wordes that Christe sayde to them that stode ydle all daye. &c. *Tota die, id est, tota vita, in pueritia, adolescentia, in iuuentute, & in senectute, vobis nihil proficientes, proximis non subuenientes, Deo non seruientes, hostibus non resistentes, & in posterum non prouidentes,* All the daye, that is, all the life (to be ydle) in thy childehoode, in thy boyehoode, in thy youth, in thy age, nothing profitable to themselues, helpefull to their neyghbours, not seruiceable to God, not resisting their ennimies, and lesse prouiding againste the last daye. This made Seneca complayne that a great part of our lyfe perisheth, in doing nothing, a greater in doing euill, and the greatest of all ; in doing things vnprofitable. Chrysostome sayeth, that
we

Eccl. 15. 20.

Gal. 6. 10.

Ambros in Gal. c. 47. 6.

Luc. 1. 75.

Math. 20. 3. 4. 5.
Luc. 19. 22.
Mat. 25. 26.

Nic. Gorran. in Math. Cap. 20.

A good place

We must be doing *Corde, mente, ore, manu:corde credendo:mente cō-patiendo: ore confitendo: manu operando,* With heart, minde, mouth, and hande: with heart in beleeuing: with minde in pacience : with mouth in confessing: with hande in labouring. So that you may well perceyue, that to be ydle and doe no good, is against the law of God & the law of nature; as Hesiodus sayth: *Illi pariter indignā-tur, & dij & homines, quisquis otiosus,* both the Gods & men detest those that are idle: & therfore was it said openly, *Otiosos & vagos so-litus est appellare, fratres muscas, quod nihil facientes boni,* Idlers & wanderers were wont to be called friers flees, y̆ are doing no good.

YOVTH. Wil you haue no leysure times graunted vnto mā? is it not a true saying: *Quies labor ŭ remedium,* rest is the medicine of labors & wearines. Therfore breathings & refresshings frō con-tinuall labors must be had, bicause it driueth awaye irkesomnesse gottē by serious toile, & doth repaire again y̆ bodies & minds to la-bor: euē as too much bēding breaketh a bow, so to be addicted perpe-tually to labors, & neuer to refresh the minde with pastimes, must nedes cause y̆ minde not long to endure in earnest studies, & ther-fore it is said, festiual dais in old time were inuented for recreatiō.

AGE. Yes truly, I do allow of honest, moderate, & good law-full actiue exercises, for recreation & quickning of our dull minds. And where you say, that holydayes (as they are termed) were in-uēted in old time for pastimes, I think you say truth. For y̆ Pope appointed them (and not God in his word) and that only to traine vp the people in ignorance & ydlenesse, whereby halfe of the yeare & more was ouerpassed (by their ydle holydayes) in loytering & vaine pastimes, &c. in restrayning men from their handy labors and oc-cupations. S. August. speaking of the abuse of the Sabboth day, sayth: It is better to dig & go to plowe on the Sabboth day, than to be drunke, and liue ydelly: howe much more may we saye so of these festiual days, neuer appointed nor cōmanded by God? &c.

YOVTH. If you do alow of exercises and recreations, why then do you so bitterly inuey and speak against plays & pastimes?

AGE. As farre as good exercises and honest pastimes & plays doe benefite the health of manne, and recreate his wittes, so farre

*Centuria.13.
Cap.10 &
in folio.1152.*

*August in
Psalme.32.*

farre I speake not against it, but the excessiue and vnmeasurable vse thereof, taketh away the right institution thereof, and bringeth abuse and misuse, and thereby is an hinderaunce of mans obedience to Gods word (as it is seene in you this present day) and therfore they are rather chaunged into faultes and transgressions, than honest exercises for mans recreation. Therefore we must in all our pastimes remember what Cicero sayth : *Non ita generati sumus à natura, vt ad ludum & iocum facti esse videamur, sed seueritatem potius, & alia studia grauiora.* Wee are not made and brought forth into this worlde by nature, to the intent we might appeare and seeme to be created to the maintenaunce of gaming and pastymes, but we are borne to more weightie matters, and grauer studies. Therfore S.Paule sayth : Whatsoeuer ye do, do all to the glorie of God.

YOVTH. It seemeth to me, you are so precise, as if you wold make vs Stoikes, that will thus exclude pastimes and playes from vs, as we nowe vse them.

AGE. Haue you so quicklye forgotten (what I sayde euen nowe) that I did allowe of all honest, good, and lawful pastimes, for those endes and purposes wherevnto they were appointed, for mans recreation and comfort. Cicero sayth in his booke of Offices, to this effect and purpose : *Ludo autem & ioco illis quidem vti licet, sed sicut somno & cæteris quietibus, tum cum grauibus seriisq, rebus satisfecerimus,* that is : Honest games and pastimes are allowable, but we ought to vse them as we doe sleepe and other eases of the bodie, and to be taken after such time as we haue laboured inough in weightie matters, and serious affaires. As we read of the Romane Scæuola, he vsed often times to play at Tennise, onely to recreate his spirites, after hee had taken great paynes in weightie matters of the common wealth.

YOVTH. I am verye gladde that you graunt some kynde of pastime and playes, although you tye it to times, matters, and persons.

AGE. Uery good reason it be so graunted, as I haue sayde. For as Cicero sayth : *Ludendi est quidem modus retinẽdus,* I measure

sure ought to be kept in all our pastimes, as the Poet sayth: *Est modus in rebus, sunt certi denique fines. Quos vltra citraq́ nequit consistere virtus.* I pray you what measure or meane keepe you & your companions now a days, that play when you should sleepe, and sleepe when you shoulde labour? The Lorde biddeth you watch and pray, and you watch and play all night long, wherby you are not able to doe your dutie in hearing of Gods worde, receyuing of his sacramentes, praying with the congregation, nor yet able to vse your vocation and calling: whereby you prouoke and heape Gods heauy displeasure and wrath vppon you, therefore you haue greate cause to bee heartily sorye, and to repent. Mar.13.33.

YOUTH. Why sir, by my sleepe I hurt no man, for therein I thought no euill, and therefore I haue not offended, that I nede to repent me for it.

AGE. My sonne, in manye things we offende all, both in thoughts, wordes, dedes, & dreames, through corruption of our nature, therefore haue wee nede to saye with Dauid: Who can vnderstande his faultes? Clense mee from secrete faultes (O Lorde. And whereas you saye, by sleeping you hurt no man: That is not sufficient to hurt no man, but you must do good also. Dauid sayth: Eschue euill and doe good, secke peace, and ensue it. What good (I pray you) hath your sleepe and ydle pastimes done to you? which hath hindered you from all good and godly exercises. No good at all, but rather great hurte, for that you abused, and not vsed your sleepe in due time and order, by reason of your ydle nightwatching playes, and ydle wanton pastimes, to satisfie the pleasures and desires of the fleshe, and therefore you neede repentance. Hereby is inferred that generall rule, *Cuius rei est vsus, eiusdem est & abusus.* There is nothing vsed, but that also maye be abused. For God in mercie giueth vs nothing (be it neuer so good) but the deuill is presently busie to drawe vs to the abuse thereof. Iam.3.2. Mat.15.19. 1.Cor.3.5. Genes.6.5. Psal.19.12. Psal.51.7. Psal.34.14. Psal.37.27. 1.Pet.3.11. Rom.8.5.6. 7.8.13. Gal.5.19. Genes.3.6. VVis.2.25.

YOUTH. Doe not you remember that Salomon sayth: That there is nothing better than that a man shoulde be merye and re- Eccl 3.22.

ioyce in his affayres, bicause that is his portion. Wherefore then shall not wee in our youthfull dayes playe and pastime?

A G E. Salomon speaketh not there of vaine, wanton, and
ydle playes, but declareth that man by his reason can compre-
hende nothing better in this life, than to vse the giftes of God
soberly and comfortably. Also he speaketh against the greedie carefulnesse of the couetous rich men, that vse to become slaues and
bondmen to their mucke and riches (contrarie to the rule of Dauid, which he giueth, saying: If riches encrease, sette not your
heartes thereon). A little before the place by you recited, he sayth:
I knowe that there is nothing good in them, but to reioyce and do
good in his lyfe. To that ende was it spoken of the wyse man a-
gainst couetousnesse, *Auaro semper deest quod habet, quàm quod
non habet,* The rich man lacketh that which he hath, as well as
that he hath not. Augustine sayth: *Non solum ille auarus est qui ra-
pit aliena, sed etiam ille auarus est qui cupidè seruat sua,* He is not
onely a couetous man that taketh away another mans goods, but
also he is a couetous man that greedily and niggardlye keepeth
his owne goods (from helping the poore) so that it is a manifest
token of Gods plague, when a rich man hath not a liberall hearte
to vse his riches. Augustine sayth: *Si ignem mittitur qui non de-
dit rem propriam, vbi putas mittendus est qui inuasit alienum?* If
he shall be cast and sent into fire that giueth not of his owne proper goods, where thinkest thou shall he be cast and sent that in-
uadeth and taketh away other mens?

YOVTH. Why doe you speake so much to mee of this couetousnesse, I am not rich, and therfore not couetous.

A G E. You are herein deceyued. For Christ in his law saith:
Thou shalte not couet nor lust: whereby he doth declare that a
greedy mynded man (although he haue no riches) may be, and is
a couetous man. So that riches (whiche is the gifte of God) is
not cause of couetousnesse, but the filthye desire and insatiable
mynde and heart of manne, and also his greedy desire to haue.
Therefore Paule sayth: The desire of mony, he sayth not simply

Psal.61.10.

Ecele.3.12.

August.

*August. de
verb. Apost.
Serm.20.*

Exo.20.17.
Rom.7.7.

Psal.75.6.
1.Sam.2.7.

1.Tim.6.10

ply (mony) but the (deſire) is the rote of all euill, whiche whyle ſome luſted after (he ſayeth luſted) they erred from the faith. A-gaine : They that will be riche, fall into temptation, and ſnares, and into many fooliſhe and noyſome luſtes , which drowne men in perdition and deſtruction . So that wee ſee, it is the luſt and will, and not the riches *per ſe*, that doth make vs couetous men. Auguſtine ſayeth : *Tolle ſuperbiam , & diuitiæ non nocebunt,* *Auguſt. in Serm.29.* Take away pride and vaineglorie,and then riches will not hurt. *Non enim* (ſayth Theophilact) *diuitiæ nocent, ſed ſolicitudines ea-* *Theophil.in Luc.cap.7.* *rum*,Riches hurt not,but the carefulneſſe of them . Chriſoſtome alſo ſayth : *Non eſt pauper, non eſt , inquam, qui nihil habet , ſed* *Chriſoſt in Epiſt.ad Phil. cap.1.* *qui multa concupiſcit : viciſsim, non eſt diues qui multa poſsidet, ſed qui nullius eget. &c. Voluntas hominum & diuites faciunt & pauperes, non pecuniarum vel abundantia, vel defectus*, that is to ſaye : He is not a poore man I ſaye, that hath nothing, but hee is a poore man that coueteth and luſteth : Agayne, he is not riche that hath and enioyeth muche (goodes) but hee that coueteth no other mannes (goodes) &c. the willes and deſires of menne ma-keth riche and poore, not the want, or abundance of monye. Se-neca ſayeth : *Diues eſt, non qui magis habet, ſed qui minus cupit,* *Seneca.* He is riche, not that hath much, but that coueteth leaſt. There-fore Saint Paule ſayth : Godlyneſſe is great gaine, if a man be 1.Tim.6.6. content with that he hath.&c. Whereby you ſee proued, that you and ſuch others, are couetous men.

YOVTH. Well, let this paſſe, and let vs come agayne vnto our former talke. Is it lawfull for Chriſtians to playe at all, or not ?

AGE. I haue ſayde to you my mynde herein alredy, what neede you to vrge me ſo often to tell you ?

YOVTH. I will ſhewe you the reaſon why that I doe aſke you again.

AGE. What reaſon is there that ſo moueth you to reiterate this ſo often ? Declare it.

YOVTH. I haue often times hearde & affirmed at the mouth

of certaine graue learned Diuines) that it is not lawfull for any Christian man (professing the fayth and true religion of Christe Iesu) to play at any game or pastime at all.

AGE. Although in this poynt, I am not altogither of their iudgement, yet no doubt they seeme to giue reasons for it, but yet I must needes confesse, these reasons of theirs are sifted very depe, and very harde, and maruelous precise.

YOVTH. I pray you let me heare what their reasons are, that they seeme to persuade by.

AGE. Their reasons are these. Seing (saye they) that wee must yelde account to God of the whole course of our life, and of eche particular dede thereof, they aske what account we are able to yelde to God of the time that we leese in playe? And seeing (say they) that we must forbeare euery ydle worde that God rebuketh vs for, yea, though it be neither othe nor blaspheming of the name of God, but onelye bicause it is ydle, and spoken to no purpose, howe then (say they) can we excuse our selues of all the ydle time that we spende in playing? We must doe all (say they) that we doe, be we great or small, riche or poore, to the glorye of God. And when we playe, can we saye that therein wee glorifie God. Paule (say they) willeth vs to redeme the time, which we haue lost in fonde and euill things when we were Idolaters, shall we thinke that it is lawfull for vs to leese and spende the same in playe, nowe when we are called to the glorie of God? It is sufficient for vs (sayeth Saint Peter) that we haue spent the time past of this lyfe after the lust of the Gentiles, walking in wantonnesse, lustes, drunkennesse, in gluttonie, drinking, and in abhominable Idolatries, to the ende that the rest of the time that we shall liue in this flesh, we should liue no more after the concupiscences of men, but after the will of God. There are so many duties (say they) that God by his worde requireth of vs, so manye meanes and holy exercises and occupations, to bestow our selues eyther to the glorie of God, or the profit of our neighbours, at all houres both daye and night, yea, though they were longer, and that euery daye had eight and fortie houres. But in stede of bestowing

Math 12.36.

1.Cor.19.32.

Ephe.5.16.

1.Pet.4.3.

stowing our selues in holye exercises ; and better businesses, wee spende away our time in playing, therefore it is intollerable, and by no meanes lawfull for any man that calleth himselfe a Christian, to play. There is the reading of the worde of God, and other good bookes, there is comforting the sicke, visiting prisoners, relieuing the nedy, and also the occupations that ech man hath in his estate and particular calling: all the whiche, with other lyke exercises, are expresslye commaunded vs by the worde of God, and we can scarce finde in our heartes to doe anye of them, and yet can we bestowe (say they) so long time in playing. Certainly all these things well considered, we cannot perceyue (say they) howe it shoulde be seemely, or lawfull for a Christian to lose any time, be it neuer so little, in play. Saint Ambrose (say they) doth generallye condemne all kinde of playe. As also Saint Chrysostome.

Math.25.35
36.

Amb.lib.1.
offic.cap.23.
etiam in
Psal.118.
Chrisost.in
Mat.hom.6.

YOVTH. I promise you they go very neare.

AGE. Although they do, yet for my parte I will not bee so straite or scrupulous. For I say with Saint Augustine, that it is the part of a wise man sometimes to recreate himselfe, and reioyce the minde, that he may the better away with, longer continue, and more chearefully returne to his ordinarie labour and vocation. S. Ambrose sayth: *Licet interdum honesta ioca.&c.* Honest pastimes are sometime lawfull.

Augustl.lib.
2.Musica.

Ambr.lib.1.
offic.cap.23.

YOVTH. I woulde very gladly heare your answeres to their reasons which they haue made.

AGE. My answere is this : We must make distinction betwene the ordinarie things that a Christian is bounde of necessitie to doe, and those things which are permitted, and graunted him by God for the refreshing and helping of his infirmitie, as to ease him when he is weary, to sleepe after labour, and to play after long paine. Ouid sayth : *Quid caret alterna requie, durabile non E,* The thing cannot endure that lacketh rest. And therefore the holy Scriptures (whiche are the rule of good and euill) maketh mention of playing, and alloweth Christians so to doe. Zacharie sayth : And the streetes of the citie shall bee full of boyes and girles,

Zacha 8.5

girles, playing in the streetes thereof. Also when Saint Paule sayth: Whether ye eate or drinke, or whatsoeuer else ye doe, doe all to the glorie of God. Wee maye by this worde, (whatsoeuer ye doe) vnderstande all honest recreations, which certainely is as lawfull and permitted to vs, by reason of our infirmitie, as is either eating, drinking, or sleeping, when wee haue neede thereof. And as our Lorde Iesus Christ sayeth: That man is made for the glorie of God, and therefore the Sabboth serueth for man, and not man for the Sabboth: so honest recreation is inuented for man and for his health, which maketh vs the better and more de-uout to serue God. Then to playe at honest games and pastimes, is a thing both indifferent and lawfull, and such as are lefte to Christian libertie, as Paule sayth: Brethren, ye haue bene cal-led vnto libertie: onelye vse not your libertie as occasion vnto the fleshe, but by loue serue one another: which thing must be ob-serued in any wise. Neuerthelesse, I cōfesse we ought not to abuse (through too great pleasure which we take in them) no more than to abuse any other thing of the lyke kinde. In very deede it should seeme too great a crueltie to restraine wearied natures, ouertoyled bodies, that they neyther might or durste take some recreation. For although we ought to apply al & euery our doings to ye glory of God, & edifying & helping of our neighbours, neuerthelesse whē we take our honest recreation to maintaine and preserue our vi-gour and health, or to recouer our strength, or to refreshe vp our spirites, that we may afterwarde the more cherefully and fresh-ly go about that businesse that God hath called vs vnto, and doe it the better. The same in the ende redoundeth to the glorie of God, whome we shall by this meanes be more able and readye to serue, and also to seeke our neighbours furtherance and profite. I doe not then forbid or condemne all playe, neither mislike that a faithfull Christian doe sometimes play and sport himselfe, so that such play and pastime be in lawfull and honest things, and also done with moderation.

YOVTH. Then I perceiue by you, that honest recreation, pa-stimes and playes are tollerable vnto menne, and that they maye vse

1.Cor.10.31

Marc.2.27.
Luc.6.5.
Math.12.8.

Gala.12 13.

vse and frequent it without fault, or offending God, or hurt to the profession of a true faithfull Christian.

AGE. If it be, as I haue sayd, moderately taken, for recreation sake, after some weightie businesse, to make one more fresh and agile, to prosecute his good and godly affaires, and lawfull businesse, I saye to you againe, he maye lawfullye doe it: yet I woulde demaunde one thing of thee my sonne, if thou wilt aunswere me.

YOV.H. That I will. What is it, let me heare?

AGE. What weightie affaires and graue studies haue you and your companions bene burthened withall? Hath it bene studying in your bookes, eyther in giuing counsell and aduise for gouernement of common wealths, or else in labouring and toyling in your handie craftes and vocation, for the sustentation & maintenance of your wiues and familie at home, that you should haue such neede to consume this whole night for recreation, pastime, and vaine playes?

YOVTH. I assure you good father Age, my studie is not Diuinitie, for I haue small learning, nor yet am I anye Magistrate, or labouring manne: for in no wise can I labour, I loue not to heare of it, of anye thing, muche lesse to vse it.

AGE. Your father hath the more to aunswere for, who is commanded by Gods holy worde to haue brought you vp (as S. Paule sayth) in the discipline and doctrine of the Lorde. S.Paule commendeth Timothie, that he had knowne the Scriptures of a childe, and commendeth him that he hadde learned the faith that was in him, of his grandmother Lois, and his mother Eunice. Whereby appeareth their diligence in bringing vp Timothie in godly knowledge, learning, and faythfulnesse in religion. Solon the Lawe maker among the Athenians, made a lawe that the childe (whose father neuer regarded to bring vppe his sonne in anye good learning or exercyse) shoulde not be bounde to succour or reliene his father in anye respecte, in what neede soeuer hee were in. Aristotle was demaunded, what the learned differed

Luc.16.3.
Prou.10.4.
Cap.21.25.
Cap.22.13.

Deut.6.7.
Ephes.6.7.
Eccles.7.6.
2.Tim.3.15.

2.Tim.1.5.

Plutarch.

Aristotle.

from

from the vnlearned : answered, *Quæ viui à mortuis,* As liuing men
Diogenes. do differ from the deade. Therfore Diogenes said well: Learning
and good letters, to yong men bringeth sobrietie : to olde menne
comfort: to poore men riches : to rich men an ornament, &c. Not
without iust cause did Chrisostome saye : Fathers are louing to
the bodies of their children, but negligent & hatefull to their soules.
Ec.30.9.10 Which is the cause that Ecclesiasticus sayeth : If thou bring vp
thy sonne delicately, he shall make thee afrayd : if thou play with
him, he shall bring thee to heauinesse. Laugh not with him, least
thou be sorie with him. &c. And where you say, you cannot labor,
I tell you plainelye, then are you not worthy to eate or drinke.
2.Thes.3.10
Ephe.4.28. For he (sayeth Saint Paule) that will not labour, ought not to
eate, that is to say, sayth a learned man, *Nolite istos otiosos alere,*
Math.Place. *sed fame eos ad laborem cogite,* Nourish not among you these ydle
Illyricus in
2 Thes.cap.3 loytering persons, but compell them with very hunger to labour:
wherby you may learn, ÿ none ought to liue ydelly, but should be
Ephe.4.28. giuen to some vocation or calling to get his liuing withall, that
Thom.de A- he maye doe good vnto others also. Thomas de Aquine sayeth :
quino in 2.
Thes.cap.3. *Qui nõ habet exercitium, vel officij, vel studij, vel lectionis, periculosè*
viuunt otiosi, They that haue no exercise, eyther of office, studie, or
reading, these liue daungerously that liue ydellye. Ecclesiasticus
Eccl.33.26. therfore sayth : Sende thy seruant to labour, that he go not ydle :
Cato. for ydlenesse bringeth much euill. Cato sayth : *Homines nihil a-*
gendo, discunt male agere, Men in doing notting, but be ydle, do
Genes.3.15. learne to doe euill. Adam was put (by God) in Paradise, it is added, that he might dresse it, and keepe it. Teaching vs, that God
Genes.3.19. woulde not haue man ydle, though as yet there was no neede to
labour. Also God sayde vnto Adam (after his fall:) In the sweate
Psal.128.2. of thy face thou shalt eate breade. Dauid sayth : Thou shalte eate
Prov.10.17. the labors of thine owne handes. Salomon sayeth : A slouthfull
hande maketh poore, but the hande of the diligent maketh riche.
You, and such as you are, esteeme your selues happie and blessed
which may liue in wealth and ydlenesse. But the holy ghost (as
you haue heard) approueth them blessed ÿ liue of the meane profit
of their owne labours. So that it appeareth, of all things, ydlenesse

nesse is most to be eschued and auoyded of all men (especiallye of those that professe the Gospell of Christ) bicause it is the foun-tayne and well-spring whereout is drawne a thousande mis-chiefes: for it is the onely nourisher and mayntainer of all filthi-nesse, as whoredome, theft, murder, breaking of wedlocke, per-iurie, Idolatrie, Poperie, &c. vaine playes, filthy pastimes, and drunkennesse. Not without cause did Ecclesiasticus saye, that ydlenesse bringeth much euill. *Otium fuge vt pestem* (sayeth Bul-linger) Flee ydlenesse, as thou wouldest flee from the plague of pestilence. *Otium enim omne malum edocuit,* Idlenesse teacheth all euill and mischiefe. Bonauenture sayth: *Otiositas magister nuga-rum est, & nouerca virtutum,* Idlenesse is the maister of fables and lies, and the stepdame of all vertue. So Ambrose sayth: *Pe-riculosa otia secura esse virtuti,* This secure ydlenesse is most dan-gerous that can be to vertue. Therefore my sonne doe according to the olde Prouerbe, *Qui fugit molam, fugit farinam.*

Eccl.32.26.
Bullinger.in decad.3.ser.3
Theophila.in 1.Tim.cap.1.
Bonauent.in li.meditatio-ne vit.Christ

Salomon reproueth such ydle persons as you are, by sending them to the Ant, saying: O sluggarde, go to the Ant, beholde hir wayes, and be wyse, for she hauing no guyde, gouernour, nor ruler, prepareth hir meate in the summer, and gathereth hir foode in the Haruest. Teaching hereby, that if the worde of God cannot instruct vs, nor persuade vs, yet wee shoulde learne at the little Ant, to labour and prouide for our selues, and not to burthen o-thers, as Saint Paule sayth: If there be any that prouideth not for his owne, and namely for them of his housholde, he denyeth the faith, and is worse than an infidell. Agayne he sayeth: Lette him that stole, steale no more: but let him rather labour and work with his hands the thing which is good, that he may haue to giue vnto him that needeth. Howe is it then, that man shameth not to liue a trifling, and an ydle loyterer, considering howe painful-y and busilye the poore Ant toyleth in the Summer, gathering hir prouision and store for the Winter, and also hauing such ma-nifest precepts in holy Scripture, to instruct him, as you heare of Saint Paule himselfe. Therfore he put that precepte to auoyde theft, to moue the Ephesians to labour, for that ydlenesse maketh

Proue.6.6.
7.8.
Cap.30.25.
1.Tim.5.8.
Ephe.4.28.

one to consume his owne goods and treasures, whereby commeth pouertie, of that issueth out deceyt, from thence commeth thefte: he addeth a reason why he should labour, not onelye to succour himselfe, but those also that haue neede. He biddeth them simply to worke, but sayth worke that is good, that is to saye, that worke and vocation which God hath ordeyned and appoynted, which is good and profitable to men. A learned father sayth hereupon, *Prohibens prauas ac inutiles artes, vt sunt histrionum, prastigiatorum, Magorum, Astrologica, & alia omnes diuinationes, aliaq́, curiosa diuersorum generum :* Forbidding (by Paules wordes) euill and vnprofitable artes, as of Enterludes, Stage playes, Jugglings, and false sleyghts, Witchecraftes, Speculations, Diuinations, or fortune tellings, and all other vayne and naughtie curious kynde of artes. Whereby we haue to note, with what kinde of labour and exercise we ought to get our liuings. For if it bee by these or such like wayes and meanes, it is most detestable and abhominable before God and man ; and cannot escape without greate punishment, vnlesse they repent, and so turne from their wickednesse.

YOVTH. Is there no remedy but that we must get our liuing with our owne labour and trauell ?

AGE. There is no remedie, for the Lorde hath commanded it, and therefore it must be done, hee hath so decreed it, as Job sayth : A man is borne to trauell, as the sparkes to flee vpward. Dauid sayth also : Man goeth forth to his worke, and to his labour vntill the euening. Neyther are we borne to our selues onely, but to others also. Plato sayth : *Homines hominum causa ess generatos,* Eche man was borne and brought into this world for others sake, as one man to helpe another. Cicero sayth : *Non nobis solum nati sumus, ortusq́, nostri partem patria vindicat, partem amici. &c.* Wee are not borne and brought into this worlde, to our selues only, for owne sake, but also for others, for part of our birth and being, our countrie doth chalenge, and the other part our parents and frendes doe require. For otherwise, *Homo homini lupus est,* A man is a wolfe to a man, that is, a deuourer on

Matth. Flacc. Illyricus in Ephe. cap. 4.

Iob. 5. 7.
Psal. 104. 23
Act. 20. 34.
Ephe. 4. 28.
1 Cor. 12. 25
2 Thes. 3. 8.
2 Thes. 4. 12

Plato.

Cic. lib. 1. de officijs.

Gal. 5. 15.

of another. Therfore let vs labour diligently in good exercises, that we may haue to minister to the needy brethren, remembring alwayes what is sayde : It is a blessed thing to giue, rather than to receyue.

Thus you may perceyue throughlye howe commendable the labouring man is, and howe detestable and odious the loyterers and ydle persons are in any common wealth : *Otiosos & vagos solitus est appellare, fratres muscas, quod nihil facientes boni*, Ydlers and wanderers were wont to be called Friers flies, which neuer doe any good. Teaching hereby that Popishe friers were and are but ydlers and loytering vagabondes, good for nothing, but euen as flies flie abroade vpon all mennes meate, to fill themselues of other mens trauels : euen so doe they. For they go ydelly a limiting abroade, liuing vpon the sweate of other mens trauels. Against such ydle Friers and Monkes, Saint Augustine wrote a booke, reprouing earnestly their ydle couetous life. &c. Seneca passing by a certaine towne called Vacia, he sawe a Citizen of Rome ydle and loytering, sayde : *Hic situs est Vacia*, Here lieth or sitteth the filth and dung of Vacia. It was truly sayde of one : *Quod otium puluinar est Satanæ*, That Idlenesse is Sathans fetherbed and pillowe that he layeth all ydlers and loyterers to sleepe vpon. The Prophet Ezechiell sayth, it was one of the sinnes of Sodom, for which God plagued them, saying : This was the iniquitie of thy sister Sodom, pryde, fulnesse of breade, and abundaunce of ydlenesse was in hir. &c. Saint Paule also reproueth a sorte of yong widowes which were in his time, and lyued ydelly, saying : Refuse the yonger widdowes, for they being ydle, haue learned to go about from house to house, yea they are not onely ydle, but also pratlers and busie bodies, speaking things whiche are not comely. Here may you see what mischiefes ensue of ydlenesse, both in men and women.

In olde time (we reade) that there was vsually caried before the mayde when she shoulde be maried, and came to dwell in hir husbandes house, a distaffe charged with flare, and a spyndle hanging at it, to the intente shee might bee myndefull to lyue

Act.10.35.

Centuria.13. ca.10.fo 152

Ezec.16.49

1.Tim.5.13.

Plin lib.8. Cap.40.
Pro.31.10.
11.12.13.

by

by hir labour. Also among the Romaynes, when anye mayde
shoulde be maried, it was alwayes solemnized vpon the working
daye, to teach what they must doe. &c. Likewise they were wont
in olde time, to haue paynted Snayles in their houses, to teache
them thereby alwayes to keepe home within their owne house,
and to see hir seruants labour in their businesse duly and truly, for
the auoyding of ydlenesse, the mother of all other vices. Saint
Hierome counsayled the mayde Demetrias to eschue ydlenesse.
And therfore when shee had made an end of hir prayers, he willed
hir to go in hande with wooll and weauing, that by such change
of workes the dayes seeme not long. He bid hir not to worke, for
that she was in any pouertie (being one of the noblest women in
Rome) but that by such occasion of working, she shoulde put out
of hir mynde foolishe and filthie imaginations and fantasies. A
certaine woman of Lacedemon taken prisoner in warre, was asked what she coulde doe: I can (sayeth she) rule an house. So
Aristotle sayth: That in keeping of an house, it is the mans part
to get, and the womans to keepe. But if she be spending & wast-
full, prodigall and ydle, Ecclesiasticus counsayle must be followed, where he sayth: Set a good locke where an euill wyfe is,
and to locke where manye handes are. *Otiositas omnium vitiorum
magistra atque origo est,* Idlenesse (sayeth Chrysostome) is the
mystres and beginning of all vice and wickednesse. Cato sayth:
*Segnitiem fugito, quæ vita ignauia fertur, Nam cùm animus lan-
guet, consumet inertia corpus,* as if he should saye: A slothfull and
ydle life is to be fled, for when the mynde is vnlustie, then ydlenesse consumeth the bodie.

    Idlenesse moste deleftable to the fleshe, which deliteth aboue
measure in sloth, litherneffe, ceasing from occupation, sluggish-
nesse, and heauinesse of mynde, and it hath a desire to be doing of
nothing, and to be voyde of all care and businesse. Yea, and this
remember my sonne Youth, that filthie lustes are chieflye nourished by excesse and ydlenesse, for thereof is the fire brande kindled,
and thereof is the oyle poured in and ministred so abundantly, as
not without cause that learned father Peter Martyr sayd: *Quam-*

uix

ui autem otium alat alioqui multa mala, nihil tamen aut facilius   P. Martyr in
aut magis alit, quàm libidinem, that is : Although ydlenesse other-   comment.in
wise nourisheth many euils, notwithstanding she nourisheth no-   2.lib. Sam.
thing more easie than sensualitie, and vnlawfull lust (of whore-   cap.12.
dome) therfore was it sayde of that wittie Poet :

    Quæritur Ægisthus quare sit factus Adulter.   Ovid.
    In promptu causa est : desidiosus erat.

        That is :
  It is asked wherefore Egisthus
    was Idulter made :
  The cause is playne, and quickly knowne :
    since he with sloth was cladde.

YOVTH. I perceyue the blinde catcheth manye a flie. For as
Christ sayth : He that walketh in the darke, knoweth not whither   Ioh.12.35.
he goeth. And Saint Paule sayde, that hee knewe not lust had
bene sinne, except the Lawe had sayde : Thou shalte not lust.   Rom.7.7.
Euen so may I say, that I had not knowne that Idlenesse had
bene such a detestable sinne as it is, except God had opened this to
me by the meanes of you. Nor yet that Satan thereby vseth to
seduce and bring vs from all vertue to vice, from faith to infideli-
tie, according as Ecclesiasticus sayth : Idlenesse bringeth much   Eccl.33.26.
euill : And as the saying of olde hath bene : *Otia dant vitia.*

A G E. It is the waye and practise that Satan vseth to steale
into our hearts, that he may possesse vs, as Christ sayth : While   Math.13.25.
man slept, there came his enimie (Satan) and sowed tares amõg
the wheate, &c. As we see in king Dauid : when he was yong, he   Psal.132.3.
exercised himselfe in preparing a house for the Lorde, and sayde: 4.5.
I will not enter into the tabernacle of mine house, nor come vpon my bed : nor suffer mine eyes to sleepe, nor myne eye lyddes
to slumber, vntill I finde out a place for the Lorde, an habitation
for the mightie God of Iacob. After, when he began to be yole, it
is sayde in the booke of Samuel, that Dauid went not vppe with
Ioab his Captaine, but sent him, and all his seruants with him,   2.Sam.11.1.
against the children of Ammon, to besiege Rabbath. But (sayth   2.3.
the text) Dauid remained in Ierusalem, and fell to lye ydelly vp-

      you.

pon his bed at noone, or euening tyde, and rose vp and walked vppon the roofe of his pallace, and from the roofe he saw Bethsheba,
Uriah the Hittites wife washing of hir selfe, and she was beautifull to looke vpon. &c. and Dauid sent for hir, and she came vnto
him, and he lay with hir, and gate hir with childe. &c. By this
example you maye see the daungerous falles that Gods childrē
fall into by this detestable bice of ydlenesse. And therefore that old
saying by you alledged, is moste true, *Otia dant vitia,* Idlenesse
bringeth and gathereth (wheresoeuer she entreth) all maner bices
and wicked sinnes. Ambrose hath a prety apt similitude to set forth
the nature of Satan vnto vs, and also his sleightes and craftie
practises to deceyue vs, to the ende we thereby may the better a-
uoyde his subtilties.

YOVTH. I praye you good father Age, declare it to mee,
that I may learne somewhat thereby to auoyde that wycked
enimie.

Ambros.in
Hexameron
Lib.5.cap.8.
A G E. The similitude is of a Crabbe, and of an Oyster, as
thus: The Crab (sayth Ambrose) deliteth very much to eate of
the meate of Oysters, but for that they (Oysters) are so strongly
and well fenced with two harde shelles, which he cannot breake
by strength, therfore he wayteth diligently to bring the Oysters
out of the water, into the hote sunne. Whiles the Oysters open
with the sunne, and with the ayre and winde, the Crab presently
putteth a little stone into the Oyster as he gapeth, whereby hee
cannot close or bring togither againe his shelles, then afterwarde
the Crab without daunger putteth in his clawes, and deuoureth
the flesh at his pleasure. Euen so (sayth he) when men are giuen
to ydlenesse, and open their mindes vnto pleasures, the Deuill
commeth, and casteth into our mindes and hearts, filthie cogita-
tions, in such sort, that our shell which before did defende vs, cannot be drawne close togither againe, then full easily doth he deuour vs cleane.

YOVTH. I promise you this is a proper similie verye aptly
applied by S. Ambrose, yet I pray you let me a litle further trouble you about this matter of ydlenesse.

A G E,

AGE. It shall be no trouble to mee, saye on in the name of God, what you haue to demaunde, and I will aunswere you as God shall giue me leaue and knowledge.

YOVTH. You haue hertofore mightily beaten downe all ydlenesse, affirming also that God detesteth it, and yet (by your patience) I doe reade in the Law, that God himselfe commaundeth vs to be ydle, saying (in the fourth commandement) The seuenth day is the Sabboth of the Lord thy God : in it thou shalt doe no manner of worke, thou, nor thy sonne, nor thy daughter, nor thy man seruant, nor thy mayde, nor thy beast, nor the straunger that is within thy gates. &c. Whereby it appeareth that the Lord alloweth of ydlenesse. &c. *Exo.20.10.*

AGE. You must learne to distinguish this word (Ydlenesse) as Saint Augustine teacheth you, saying : *Est otium desidiæ, & otium cogitationis,* that is : There is ydlenesse of sitting still, and there is ydlenesse of meditations. Uerye well noted also was it of Brentius, saying : *Est otium ignauum, quo inertes parant se non ad negotia, sed ad delicias & voluptates. Est otium honestum & necessariū, quo boni viri reddunt sese aptiores ad negotia & vocationes suas sectandas. Tale otium non solum suasit, sed mandauit Deus in lege, dum instituit Sabbatum, & iubet in eo non hominem tantum, verumetiam iumenta quiescere. Otiemur non ad luxum, quod impij & ignaui solent, sed ad pietatem. &c.* That is : There is a beastly and slothfull ydlenesse, which ydle persons get to themselues, not for labours, but for pleasures and delites. There is also an honest and a necessarie ydlenesse, whereby good men are made more apte and ready to doe their labors and vocations whereunto they are called. This kinde of ydlenesse, God doth not onely persuade, but also commaundeth it in his lawe, in that he appoynted the Sabboth day, and commaunded that in it, not only manne shoulde rest, but the beasts also. Let vs then be ydle, not for carnall pleasures, as the wicked and vngodlye are wonte, but for godlynesse and vertues sake. &c. Maister Bullinger also sayeth : *Sabbatum à Deo institutum est, non propter otium per se. Otium enim Deus nusquam per se approbat : proinde otium Sabbati commendantur* *August.de vera religione.Cap.35.*

Brentius in Luc.Cap. Homil.55.

Bullinger.in Ierem.ca.17?

propter

propter aliud, nimirum propter diligens religionis studium: ideò enim feriandum præcipitur à laboribus manuriis, vt hoc totum tempus impendamus exercitio religionis, that is: The Sabboth day was appointed of God, not for Idlenesse simplye. Idlenesse of it selfe is no where allowed of God: therefore the ydlenesse of the Sabboth day was commended for another purpose, that is, for the studie and diligent desire of religion. Therefore he commaunded to rest from our handie labors, that wee might bestowe all that time in the exercise of religion. It is likewise in the very same commaundement sayde: that God rested the seauenth day &c. Shall we conclude with the heretikes, that God sitteth ydelly in heauen, and hath no care of his creatures by his heauenly prouidence, nowe he hath once created them? (God forbid.) This rest of God (as the Scripture testifieth, was *à creatione, sed non à gubernatione,* it was from creating, but not from gouerning and ordering them. For he doth alwayes by his power sustaine them, by his prouidence gouerne and rule them, and by his goodnesse nourishe them. Wee must rest therefore from handie and bodily workes, but we must not cease from such works as pertaine vnto the true worshipping of God. This seruice among the fathers, were vsed in iiij. things, that is. First in reading, interpreting, and hearing of Scriptures. Secondly, in prayers publike and priuate, in celebrating and receyuing of Sacraments. Thirdly, in collecting and gathering for the poore and indigent. Fourthly, in visiting and distributing to the poore, and making of peace and vnitie among neighbours where any controuersie was.

YOVTH. Then I perceyue we must refrayne from all other labors vpon the Sabboth (except those which you haue specified) and so of necessitie we ought not to vse any labour or work what neede or necessitie soeuer there shoulde be.

AGE. You must note that the Sabboth was made for man, and not man for the Sabboth, and therefore is the sonne of man Lorde ouer the Sabboth: The Sabboth was instituted of God to conserue man, and not to destroy man, and therfore the Sabboth is to be dispensed withall, as often as it shall be through our necessitie,

Marginal notes:
Exo.20.11.
Actes.11.29.
1.Cor.16.2.
Math.12.8.
Luc.6.6.
Marc.3.1.

fitie, fafetie, oʒ health, fo required. Of the which thing our Sauiour Chʒiſt diſputeth in Mathew and Luke, foʒ in ſuch things ⟨Luc.6.9.⟩
the libertie of the Chʒiſtians doth conſiſt. And wheras the Pʒieſts ⟨Marc.3.4.⟩
and Leuites were exerciſed openly in ſlaying of beaſtes in the ⟨Rom.14.6.⟩
Temple, ſcumming, ſeething, and burning them, pʒepared foʒ
their ſacrifices, & were not counted guiltie of the bʒeache of the ⟨Num.28.9.⟩
Sabboth daye. In lyke ſoʒt it ſhall be lawfull to pʒepare meate ⟨Mat.12.5.⟩
foʒ our neede on the Sabboth day, and to feede the body. Mat-
tathius thought it had not bene lawfull to fight vppon the Sab- ⟨1. Macha.2.⟩
both day: but when he conſidered the ende of the Sabboth, howe ⟨40.41.⟩
it was oʒdeyned to pʒeſerue, and not to deſtroye, willed all men
to make batteil vpon the Sabboth day, bicauſe they might not die
all of them as their bʒethʒen did which were murthered by their
enimies. So it is lawfull vpon the Sabboth daye, to heale the ⟨Luc.6.9.⟩
ſicke, to viſit the ſicke and pʒiſoners, to ſuccour the needy, to fight ⟨Math.11.12⟩
in defence, that we may pʒeſerue the creature of God. If it bee ⟨Luc.13.15.⟩
lawfull (as Chʒiſt ſayth) to dʒawe a beaſt out of a ditch oʒ myʒe
on the Sabboth day, why is it not lawfull on the Sabboth daye
to ſaue a houſe that is ready to fall, oʒ a burning, oʒ to mooʒe a
ſhip faſter that is ready to runne againſt the rockes ? Why is it
not lawfull on the Sabboth day to gather togither coʒne oʒ haye
which hath layne abʒode a long time, and to ſaue it, leaſt it ſhuld
thʒough the iniurie and foʒce of the weather, and hie floudes and
ſpʒings of waters, be vtterly deſtroyed ?

YOVTH. If it be ſo, as you haue ſayde, why then did Mo- ⟨Num.15.32.⟩
ſes and Aaron commaunde the congregation to ſtone to death ⟨35.36.⟩
that man that was founde gathering ſtickes vpon the Sabboth ⟨Exo.31.13.⟩
day ? And why doth God thʒeaten ſuch plagues on thoſe that ca- ⟨14.⟩
rie any burthen on the Sabboth day ? ⟨Iere.17.21.⟩

AGE. In that he was ſtoned to death, was not ſimplye foʒ
gathering of ſtickes, oʒ that he did this of neceſſitie, oʒ of ignorance and ſimplicitie (as ſome ſuppoſe) but foʒ that he did it of
ſet purpoſe, contumeliouſly, obſtinately, and ſtubboʒnely didde
bʒeake and violate this commaundement of God: Oʒ as it were
in ſpite of Moſes Gods magiſtrate, woulde doe this in the open

face of all people, teaching others (by his example) to do the like,
therfoze Moses commaunded to stone him to death accozding to
the lawe. Foz if he had done it of ignozance, necessitie, and simplicitie, then should not he haue died (as it is expzessed in the very same chapter) but certaine burnt offerings had bene offered to
the Lozde foz him. &c. But (sayeth the Lawe) if anye person
doeth pzesumptuously despise the wozde of the Lozde, and bzeake
his commaundements, he shall be vtterly cut off from among the
people. &c. Whereby you may perceyue that he was put to death
foz his contempt against the Lozde. And foz that cause Lyzah
supposeth this man was first kept in pzison, vntill it was tryed
out whether he did it contemptuously oz ignozantly. And foz that
God sayth: (He that defileth the Sabboth, shall die the death. &c.)
It was repeated of God, foz a speciall poynte, teaching hereby,
that the whole keeping of the lawe standeth in the true vse of the
Sabboth, which is, to cease from our wozkes, and to obey the
will of God. Foz the obseruation of the Sabboth doth extende as
well vnto the faith we haue in God, as vnto the charitie of oure
neighbozs. Also by this example we see the authozitie of the magistrate, howe it is not onelye to punishe matters and faultes
committed agaynst the seconde table: but also foz faultes and
trespasses committed against the first table, foz matters touching
religion. So S. Augustine sayth: *In hoc Reges sicut eis diuinitus*
præcipitur Deo seruiunt in quantum Reges sunt, si in suo regno bona
iubeant, mala prohibeant, non solùm quæ pertinent ad humanam so-
cietatem, verùm etiam quæ ad diuinam religionem, that is: In this
Kings, as it is commaunded them of God, doe serue God as
Kings, if in their kingdome they commaunde good things, and
fozbid euill things, not onely those things which pertayne to hu-
maine societie, but also to all godly religion. Some read of Na-
buchodonosoz, howe he serued God, when he fozbad by a terrible
law, all men dwelling in his kingdome, from blaspheming God.
So likewise we may reade of that godly king Ezechias, how he
destroyed the temple of the Idols. &c. Whereby we see that Pzin-
ces may lawfully deale in matters of religion, and also may law-

fully

Num.15.24

27

Leui.4.27.

Lira in Num
cap.15. et
Glo.ordi.

Exod.31.14

Caluinus in
Exod.cap.15

August.cont
pra Crescen.

Dan.3.29.

2.Reg.18.4

Deute.13.5.

fully put to death open and obstinate Papistes and heretikes, that holde any false doctrine manifestly against the worde and commaundement of God. Whereas Christ sayth: Let both the tares and wheate growe togither vntill the Haruest. &c. apperttayneth nothing vnto the Magistrate, but vnto the Minister onely. &c. As for the place of Ieremie, you shall note, that he goeth aboute to shewe the Iewes the right keeping of the Lawe. For by naming the Sabboth day, he comprehendeth the thing that is thereby signified: for if they transgressed in the ceremonie, they must needes be culpable of the rest, which is meditating the spiritual Sabboth or rest, hearing of Gods worde, and resting from worldly trauels. And doth also declare, that by the breaking of this one commaundement, he maketh them transgressors of the whole lawe, forasmuch as the first and seconde table are therein contayned, that is, as I haue sayde before, fayth towardes God, and charitie towardes our neyghbors: and not for our owne fantasie, gaine, and pleasure, we shoulde go about our owne businesse, and leaue our duty towards God, and giue our selues to al maner ydlenesse, and Ethnicall sportes and pastimes, as is nowe vsed too muche amongst vs. That day is most holy, in the which we must apply and giue our selues vnto holy workes and spirituall meditations. For if we doe but rest (in the Sabboth day) from the works of the bodie, then do we take ý like rest as beasts do, and not as the faithfull doe. Saint Hierome to this sayth: *Non sufficit à malis esse otiosum, si quis fuerit à bonis otiosus,* It is not ynough for man to rest and cease from euil things, if a man be ydle from good things. Likewise Saint Augustine sayth: *Quod in otio non debet esse iners vacatio, sed aut inquisitio veritatis, aut inuentio,* that is: In ydlenesse sluggish rest ought to be away, and when he is at rest, there ought to be either inquisitio of the truth, or inuention of the same.

YOVTH. What doth this worde Sabboth signifie?

AGE. It signifieth in Hebrue, quietnesse or rest.

YOVTH. Howe many Sabboths are there?

AGE. Three. The first is corporall: to cease from our bodily labours. Seconde is spirituall: to cease from our sinne. Thirde

Mat.13.30.

Beza de pu- nied. haret.

Iere.17.22.

Nehe.13.15.

Nehe.8.6 2.3.4.5.

Hieronym. Epist.17.

Essay.66.23
1.Cor.2.9.
Reue.14.13
62.22.3.4.5

is heauenly : that is after this our pilgrimage, and ende of our life, we shall keepe our Sabboth and rest in heauen with Iesus Christ for euer and euer.

YOVTH. You haue throughlye satisfied me in this point, I thank you good Father for it. Yet I pray you let me vnderstand

Mat.12.36.

what Christ meaneth by saying in S. Mathewe, that of euerye ydle worde that men shall speake, they shall giue account thereof at the daye of iudgement.

AGE. That is a sharpe saying and a true, if we shall giue account for euery ydle worde (O Lorde be mercifull to vs) what shall we doe then for our ydle and sinnefull workes. By these ydle

Hier. n.in
Math 12.

wordes, Saint Hierome vnderstandeth all that is spoken without profit to the hearers, letting passe good and gracious talke, and speake of friuolous vaine things, full of scurrilitie and baw-

Bulling.in
Math.12.

drie.&c. Maister Bullinger sayth : Hereby is forbidden all lyes, vanities, and whatsoeuer springeth of the affections of the fleshe.

Muscul.in
Math.12.

Maister Musculus sayeth : That Christ hereby declareth, that we shall not giue accountes to God onely for deedes, but also for wicked wordes, not onely for vaine wordes, but for ydle wordes : if for ydle wordes, what for hurtfull wordes? what for lyings? what for slaunderings? what for cursings? what for feastings and mockings? what for periuries, shall be done hereafter to those

Psal.139.4.

at the daye of iudgement? Wee see hereby, that there is not a worde in our tongue, but the Lorde knoweth them wholy alto-

Psal.141.3.

gither. Not without great cause therefore did Dauid pray vnto the Lord, that he would set a watch before his mouth, to keepe the

1.Cor.15.33
Ephe.5.3.4

doore of his lippes. Bicause (sayth Paule) euill speakings corrupt good maners. Saint Paule sayth : that fornication and all vncleannesse or couetousnes must not be once named among vs, as it becommeth Saints. Neither filthinesse, neither foolish talking, neither iesting, which are things not comelye, but rather

Collo.4.6.
Ephe.4.29

giuing of thanks. Let your speach be gracious alwayes, poudred with salt. He sayth also : Let no corrupt communication proceede out of your mouthes, but which is good to the vse of edifying, that it may minister grace to the hearers : In fine therefore

foze he concludeth to the Colossians, thus : Whatsoeuer ye shall doe, in worde oz deede, doe all in the name of the Lozde Iesus, giuing thanks to God euen the father by him, *o quàm sanctum est os, vnde semper cælestis erumpunt eloquia,* O (sayth Augustine) howe holy is that mouth whereout commeth alwayes heauenlye speaches. Let them take heede therefore which speake what they list, saying with the wicked in the Psalme : With our tongue we will preuaple, our lippes are our owne, who is Lozde ouer vs ? But (sayth the Prophet) the Lozde will cut off all flattering lippes, and the tongue that speaketh proud things. Dauid asketh, what the deceitfull tongue bzingeth vnto himselfe ? oz what doth it auayle him ? Salomon sayeth : that life and death are in the power of the tongue, and they that loue it, shall eate the fruite thereof.

Collo.3.17.
Augustad
fraires in
Erem.ser.3.
Psal.12.4.
Psal.12.3.
Psal.120.3.
Iam.3.5.6.7
Prou.18.21.
Ecc 5.14.15

YOVTH. Is it not lawfull then to vse any kinde of ieasting oz mery talke, when companies are gathered togither to make them merie withall ?

AGE. Yes, so that your talke and ieasting be not to the dis= glozie of Gods name, oz hurt to your neighbour, you maye. Foz there are diuers examples in the Scriptures of pleasant talke, which is also godlye, as Eliah ieasted with Baals Prophetes, saying : Crie loude, foz he (meaning Baall the Idoll) is a God, eyther he talketh oz pursueth his enimies, oz is in his iourney, oz it may be that he sleepeth, and must be awaked. &c. When honest iesting (to good honest endes) be vsed, it is tollerable. Therefore Paule sayeth not simplye (Ieasting) but addeth, whiche are things not comely, meaning ieasting that is full of scurrilitie and filthinesse.

Collo.3.17.
1.Reg.18.27
Esa.44.11.
12.
Baruc.6.13
14.15.16.17.
18.19.20.
2.Cor.12.13.

YOVTH. Well, let this passe, and let vs come againe to our talke that we had befoze, which was, that you wente aboute to dziue me to labour foz my liuing, and that euerye man shoulde walke in his vocation, to get his bzeade in the sweate of his face. Well, I tell you plaine, Playes must be had, and we will haue them, say you to the contrarie what you lyst.

AGE. Salomon sayth: He that loueth pastimes, shall be a

Prou.21.17.
Cap.20.13.

G.iij.   pooze

Eccle.10.18. poore man.&c. Agayne he ſayth : By ſlothfulneſſe the roofe of the houſe goeth to decay, and by the ydleneſſe of the handes, the houſe droppeth through : againe, a diligent hande maketh riche, but a ſlothfull hande maketh poore. He that tilleth his lande, ſhall bee ſatiſfied with breade : but he that followeth the ydle, is deſtitute of defence.&c.

Prou.10.4.

Prou.12.11.

Math.6.25. 26.28.   *YOVTH.* And it pleaſe you ſir, Chriſte biddeth vs not to bee carefull for our liues, what we ſhall eate and drinke, and ſayeth that the Lillies of the fielde labour not, neyther ſpinne, yet Salomon was neuer arrayed like vnto them. And alſo that the birdes doe not ſowe, reape, nor carie into the barne.&c. We are bidden alſo not to care for to morowe, for the morowe ſhall care for it ſelfe, the day hath inough with his owne griefe.&c. By this I doe gather, that labour is not ſo neceſſarie, or that wee ſhoulde haue any care, but to caſt all our care vpon the Lord, for he careth for vs. And therefore what neede we to labour?

1.Pet 5.7.

   AGE. Chriſt doth not here clerely forbidde all kinde of care, but onely that which commeth of a diffidence and miſtruſte in Gods prouidence. You muſt conſider, that there are two ſortes of cares. Firſt is that which is ioyned with fayth, by honeſt labour to prouide for his familie things honeſt and neceſſarie. For otherwiſe (ſayth Saint Paule) he denieth the fayth, and is worſe than an infidell. The ſeconde is that, which riſeth of doubt or deſpayre, of an Epicuriall care and miſtruſt in the Lorde, and this kynde of care is here by Chriſt reproued. For Chriſts words teach vs, that God will prouide for euery day, that that ſhall bee neceſſarie, though wee doe not encreaſe the preſent griefe thereof by the carefulneſſe howe to liue in time to come. And here you muſt note and marke, that Chriſt our Sauiour doth not ſay: Labour not for meate and drinke, but be not carefull (ſayth he:) he doth not prohibite or forbid labour, but Heatheniſhe and an Epicuriall carefulneſſe : *Verum incrementum Dei non datur otioſis, ſed iperantibus ac ſeminantibus,* God giueth not increaſe to ydlers, but to them that worke and ſowe.&c. So Saint Paule ſayth : *Vnuſ- quiſque manibus ſuis laboret, vt habeat & vnde det neceſsitatem in- digenti*

1.Tim.5.8.

Muſculus in Gene.cap.26.

1.Theſ.4.11. 12.

2.Theſ.3.12

digenti.&c. Let euery manne labour and worke with his hands, that hee maye haue wherewithall to giue them that suffer neede. And if your reason did holde true, then we should neede neuer to pray for our necessities. For that Christ sayth: Your heauenlye father knoweth what neede we haue before we aske. Againe, bee not carefull what you shall eate or drinke.&c. Shall we therefore conclude hereupon, that we must not pray or care litle or nothing what we eate or drinke, whether it bee poyson, carrion, or anye vnwholesome thing. No man is so foolishe, I trowe, so to doe. And as for the birdes that doe not sowe or reape, and the Lillies that labour not, neyther spinne.&c. Although I may saye to you, *Legibus enim viuimus, non exemplis,* Wee liue by lawes, and not by examples. Yet S. Augustine shall aunswere you in this point, (who hauing iust occasion to reproue certaine ydle Monkes that were in his dayes, which woulde not labour for their liuing, as they ought to doe, but tooke occasion (as you doe) by the example of the birdes of heauen, and Lillies of the fielde, to be altogither ydle from any labour or good exercise of their bodies, or handy oc-cupations, learning thereby to liue like the ydle Dumble Bee in the hyue, vpon the sweate and trauels of other mennes labours.) *Si vultis (inquit) imitari volucres & Lilia, cur hæc quoque illa non imitamini? Lilia non comedunt aut bibunt: aues non recondunt in crastinum, neque congregant in apothecas: neque molunt & coquūt, at vos editis & bibitis, & studiose reconditis,* that is: If you will imitate and followe the example of the birdes and Lillies (not to labour,) wherefore doe you not imitate them also in this poynte? the Lillies neyther eate nor drinke: the birdes doe not lay vppe a-gainst the morowe, neither gather togither into the Sellers: nei-ther doe they grinde corne, seeth, or boyle meate, yet you doe eate and drinke, and are carefull and diligent to lay vp in store, you do grynde corne, and seeth and boyle meate (for your vse) *Hoc enim aues non faciunt,* this the birdes (and Lillies) doe not, sayth Augu-stine. S. Chrysostome sayth: *Non dixit, nolite laborare, sed nolite solliciti esse. Ergo sollicitie esse vetamur, laborare autē iubemur. Sic enim Dominus loquens ad Adam: non dixit, cum sollicitudine facies tibi*

panem,

Math.6.8.
Math.6.32.

August.de
opere Mon-
cap.23.

Ibidem.

Chrisost.in
Math.cap.5.
homil.15.

panem, sed cum labore & sudore faciei tuæ : Ergo non solicitudini-
bus spiritualibus, sed laboribus corporalibus acquirendus est panis: Si-
cut laborantibus enim pro præmio diligentiæ, Deo præstante, panis a-
bundat: sic dormientibus & negligentibus, pro pœna negligentiæ,
Deo faciente, subducitur. &c. That is : the Loꝛde did not say, labour not, but be ye not carefull. Therefoꝛe we are foꝛbidden to be
carefull, but we are commaunded to labour, so the Loꝛde sayde
vnto Adam : he sayde not to him with carefulnesse thou shalt get
thy bꝛeade, but with the labour and sweate of thy face. Therefoꝛe
not with spirituall carefulnesse , but with coꝛpoꝛall labours our

2.Tim.2.6. bꝛeade is to be gotten, as to the labourers foꝛ the rewarde of their
diligence (by the blessing and helpe of God) their bꝛeade encrea-
2.Pet.2.13. seth : so to the slothfull and negligent, foꝛ the punishment of their
Proue.12.11. slothfulnesse & ydlenesse, God sendeth them penurie and want. &c.

Nowe my sonne, you haue hearde by Gods woꝛde, and the an-
cient Fathers, what you ought to doe, therefoꝛe learne you first to
Math.6.33. seeke the kingdome of God and his righteousnesse, and all these o-
Deut.28.1. ther things shall be ministred vnto you : that is, applye the hea-
2.3.4.5. ring of Gods woꝛde, and amende your life, foꝛ God of his owne
Iames.1.18. will begat vs with the woꝛde of truth, that we shoulde be the first
fruites of his creatures. And also to learne to walke in that voca-
Rom.12.7.8 tion, wherevnto euerye man is called , as God maye bee gloꝛi-
Math.5.16. fied, the pooꝛe members of Chꝛiste comfoꝛted, and oure selues
1.Pet.2.12. saued.
Luk.74.75.

YOVTH. By this your long discourse against ydlenesse, it se-
meth to mee, that you doe condemne hereby, all Pꝛinces, Noble
men, Magistrates, Pꝛeachers, Scholemaisters. &c. foꝛ they laboꝛ
not, noꝛ haue any handie craft to get their liuing withall.

AGE. You must note, that there are two soꝛtes of labours:
Ro.13.1 2.3. One is, of the mynde and wit : the other, of the hands and body.
1.Cor.12.28 And so the Pꝛince, Rulers, Magistrates, Pꝛeachers, Counsay-
Ephe.4.28. lers, &c. in their vocation and calling, laboureth (with great stu-
Rom.12.4. die, and industrie of mynde and witte) foꝛ the pꝛomoting of Gods
5.7.8. gloꝛie, the good gouernement and state of the Common wealth,
1.Cor.12.11. teaching and pꝛeaching to the ignoꝛant people, to keepe men in
1.Timo.2.2.   peace
Actes.2.28.
1.Pet.5.2.
1.Tim.5.17.

peace and tranquilitie, for you must not thinke, that they labour not, which doe not labour at the Plowe, Cart, or otherwise with their hands : for the eternall God hath appoynted and diuided his Church militant, for these foresayde causes into foure partes. First, into Principalitie. Seconde, into Nobilitie. Thirde, into Pastoralitie. Fourthly, into Vulgaritie. So that euery member hath his office and calling, not to be ydle, but alwayes diligent and laboursome in their vocations accordingly : therefore what-soeuer the diuersitie is, yet the profit is common, and serueth to the edification of the Church . So that it appeareth, it is no small carke and care that Princes, Rulers, Pastours. &c . haue and take continuallye , watching when others sleepe, according to this saying :

Eccle 17.17.
1.Cor.12.14
1.Pet.2.13 .
1.Tim.2.2.
Ephe.4.11.
1.Cor.12.28
Ec.38.37 34.

Non decet integram noctem dormire regentem.

Whom God hath placed to rule aright,
Ought not to sleepe a full whole night.

Iuuenall

Notwithstanding, yet wee reade in auncient hystories, that excellent men in olde time (when as they had gotten any vacant or leysure time, eyther from holy seruice, or from ciuill matters) they spent all that leysure time, eyther about husbandrie, or about the arte of a Shepehearde. For they woulde not consume the time away in ydlenesse, sumptuousnesse, gluttonie, drunkennesse, and vayne pastimes and playes . And this shall we not onely see in Abraham, Isaac, Jacob, Gedeon. &c. and other holy fathers and Apostles of Christ Jesu. &c. but also it manifestlye appeareth by the Romaine hystories, wherein appeareth that Curius and Se-ranus and such like, were elected chiefe Magistrates, when they were in the fieldes at plough tilling the grounde. It is also writ-ten that Xerxes king of Persia, in vacant time from the affayres of his Realme, he with his owne handes woulde plant innume-rable trees, which long ere he died , brought forth abundance of fruite. &c. If such men woulde spende no time ydelly, how much lesse shoulde meaner persons doe it. For as the wyse man sayth : A slothfull man is to be compared to the dung of Oxen. &c. For

Eccl.4.20

Iudge.6.11.
Act.20.34.
Ioh.21.2.
1.Thes.2.9.

Eccle.22.2.
Cap.33.26 4.

ydlenesse

ydleneſſe bringeth much euill.

YOVTH. I pray you ſhew what is ydleneſſe, and also whether ydleneſſe, be called ydleneſſe, onely in reſpect that the mynde or bodie ceaſeth from labour.

AGE. Idleneſſe is a wicked will giuen to reſt and ſlothfulneſſe, from all right, neceſſarie, godly, and profitable workes. &c. Alſo ydleneſſe is not onely of the body or mynde to ceaſe from labour, but eſpecially an omiſſion or letting paſſe negligentlye all honeſt exerciſes: for no day ought to be paſſed ouer without ſome good profitable exerciſes, to the prayſe of Gods glorious name, to our brethrens profite, and to our ſelues commoditie and learning.

YOVTH. Was there euer any lawes made againſt this kinde of ydle life, and ſharpe puniſhment appointed for ſuch ydle perſons? I pray you let me knowe it, if there were or be any.

AGE. Yes: There hath bene lawes and puniſhment from time to time appointed and ordeined for ſuch. Alexander the emperour ſayth: Foraſmuch as ydleneſſe, that is to ſay (ſayth he) ceaſing from neceſſarie occupations or ſtudies, is the ſinke which receyueth all the ſtinking chanels of vice, which once being brym full, ſodenly runneth ouer, through the whole Citie, and wyth his peſtiferous ayre infecteth a great multitude of people, ere it maye bee ſtopped and clenſed. And that notwithſtanding, the people being once corrupted and infected with this peſtilence, ſhal with great difficultie, and with long tract of time bee deliuered. And therefore he made a law: That if any one of the people had bene founde ydle, by the ſpace of one whole daye, hee ſhoulde bee whipped, and after by the Conſeruatours committed to ſome one Crafte that he was of, and for euery daye that he was ſeene to be ydle, the perſon to whome he was committed, ſhoulde (for a Monethes ſpace) ſette him to anye labour that hee pleaſed, as his ſlaue and bondman, and that no man ſhould giue him meate, or to talke with him, vnleſſe it were to chyde and rebuke him.

Draco the Lawmaker among the Athenians, made a lawe, that

Alexander part.2.queſt. 226.mem.2.

Alexand. Seuerus.

Draco.

that whosoeuer was founde an ydle person, should haue his head cut off from his bodie.

Areopagite did also vse greate diligence to search oute what arte or science euery manne had to finde himselfe withall, and those whome hee founde to be ydle, hee didde sharpelye punishe them. *Areopagite.*

The Massyliens woulde suffer, nor receyue anye manne to dwell within their Citie, that had not some Arte and facultie to get his liuing withall. For (say they) *Nullam vrbibus pestem nocentiorem esse otio,* There is no worse pestilence to a citie than ydlenesse. &c. According as Syrach sayeth: A slothfull man is to be compared to the dung of Oxen, and euerye one that taketh it vp, will shake it out of his hande: he is like a filthie stone, which euery man mocketh at for his shame. *Massyliens.* *Eccl.22.12*

Queene Elizabeth in the xiiij. and xviij. yeres of hir gracious reygne, two Actes were made for ydle vagrant and maisterlesse persons, that vsed to loyter, and woulde not worke, shoulde for the first offence haue a hole burned through the gristle of one of his eares of an ynche compasse. And for the seconde offence committed therein, to be hanged. *Queene Eli an.14. & 18*

If these and such lyke lawes were executed iustlye, truly, and seuerely (as they ought to be) without any respect of persons, fauour or friendshippe, this dung and filth of ydlenesse woulde easily be reiected and cast oute of thys Common wealth, there woulde not be so many loytering ydle persons, so manye Ruffians, Blasphemers, and Swinge Bucklers, so many Drunkardes, Tossepottes, Whoremaisters, Dauncers, Fydlers, and Minstrels, Diceplayers, and Maskers, Fencers, Theeues, Enterlude players, Cutpurses, Cosiners, Maisterlesse seruauntes, Jugglers, Roges, sturdye Beggers, counterfaite Egyptians &c. as there are, nor yet so manye Plagues to bee amongst vs as there are, if these dunghilles and filthe in Common weales, were remoued, looked vnto, and cleane caste oute, by the industrie, payne, and trauell of those that are sette in authoritie, and haue gouernemente. So Moyses sayeth:

Deut.13. That they must take the euill awaye forth of the myddes of the
Citie. &c. So sayth Publianus, *Bonis nocet, quisquis pepercerit*
malis, He is very hurtfull to the good men, whosoeuer fauoureth
and spareth the euill men. Therefore they must execute iustice,
as well vpon the proper man that is ydle, as vpon the poore man,
as well vppon one, as vpon another, that it may not be sayde:

> *Dat veniam coruis, vexat censura columbas.*
> *Crabrones abeunt, recidunt in retia muscæ.*

What faultes great men alwayes committe,
Are pardoned still, and goeth quitte.
When as the poore and simple bande,
Are vexed cruelly in the lande.
Bicause Hornets are very great,
They easily passe through the net,
When as the sillie little flye,
Is taken therein continuallye.

YOVTH. I am very glad (I prayse God) that I haue had
this talke and communication with you, good Father, I perceyue
that nothing is to be had or gotten in absenting from Sermons,
but euilnesse and losse of good doctrine and instructions, which I
haue done through vaine ydle pastimes and playes. For nowe (by
you) I vnderstande, that of ydlenesse commeth no goodnesse,
but rather the contrary. &c. Also I see and learne that euery man
(in his calling) ought to labour and get his liuing in the feare of
God, and sweate of his browes. And therefore I will henceforth
(God willing) speake no more against the worde of truth, but
Ec.4.25,26. will be ashamed of the lyes of mine owne ignorance, I will not
Dani.9.5.6. therefore be ashamed to confesse my sinnes, and will no more resist
7.8.9.10. the course of the riuer.
Lu.15.18.19.

    AGE. I am glad to heare this of you, that you are so reclai-
med, and are not ashamed to confesse your lewde life, which is a
Rom.8.26. token that Gods spirit is in you. For as you confesse: we ought
(euery man in his calling) to doe good: for in doing nothing, we
Ephe.4.23. learne to doe euill, so that you nowe flee from that vaine ydle life,
                                            which

which before you haue liued, and spent a great time therin (not-withstanding, *Nunquam serum est, quòd verum est,* that is : Ne-uer to late done, which is truly done) that will come to passe that Ouid sayth : 1.Pet.4.3.

Cyprianus.

> *Otia si tollas, periere Cupidinis arcus.*   *Ouid.*
>
> If thou flee ydlenesse,
>   Cupid hath no might :
> His bowe lieth broken,
>   his fire hath no light.

YOVTH. By what meanes shall I frame my selfe hereunto, and to redresse my former wayes, and naughtie ydle playes and pastimes, and also my wily wanton lyfe, which will be hard for me to bridle, according to that saying of Euripides.

Euripides.

> What custome we in tender youth,
>   by natures lore receaue :
> The same we loue, and like alwayes,
>   and lothe our lust to leaue.

AGE. In dede as the Prophet sayth : The waye of man is not in himselfe, neither is it in man to walke and to directe his steppes. Therefore you must with the same Prophet say : Thou hast corrected mee, and I was chastened as an untamed calfe. Conuert thou me (O Lorde) and I shall be conuerted. The paths of man are directed by the Lorde. &c. Wherewithall (sayeth Da-uid) shall a yong man redresse his wayes ? In taking hede there-vnto (sayth he) according to thy worde. For it is a lanterne vnto our feete, and a light vnto our pathes. &c. This worde will deli-uer thee (sayth Salomon) from the euill waye, and from thē that leaue the wayes of righteousnesse, to walke in the wayes of dark-nesse, which reioyce in doing euill, and delite in the frowardnesse of the wicked. Therefore walke thou in the wayes of good men, and keepe the wayes of the righteous . Therefore (sayth Saint Paule :) Bee not ouercome of euill, but ouercome euill wyth goodnesse. So that you must be nowe an earnest and continuall

Iere.10.14.

Iere.31.18.
Psal.37.23.

Psal.119.9.
105.

Prouerb.2
12.
13.
14.
20.

Rom 12.21.

bearer of Gods worde, often to pray and call vpon God through
Iesus Christ. Alwayes be you tied to some labour and businesse,
neuer giue any respit to vnhonest lusts, but with godly studies, &
honest occupations resist the pride of the flesh, and with accustomed fasting, prayers, and repentance, kepe vnder your lasciuious
life. For as S. Ierome sayth: *semper age aliquid, vt Diabolus*
adueniens semper te inueniat occupatum, non enim facile capitur à
diabolo, qui bono vacat exercitio, that is: Alwayes be doing some-
thing, that when the deuill commeth, he maye finde thee (well)
occupied: for he is not easily taken by the deuill, that applieth good
exercise. &c. You must also call to remembrance what vowe & promise you made in your baptisme: you must remember that we be al
called to godlynesse and cleannesse: you must remember ȳ short-
nesse of your time, and the vncertaintie thereof: also the paynes
of hell for the vngodly. &c. These things shall drawe you awaye
from the companies of the wicked, and make you desire the companie of the godly and vertuous men.

YOVTH. I beseech God I may folow this your good and godly counsell, I beseech you let me craue your earnest and heartie
prayers vnto God for me, that I may crucifie the flesh with the
affections and lusts thereof, and as I liue in the spirite, so I maye
walke in the spirite.

AGE. I will not fayle but pray for you, that you maye obtaine this for his mercies sake, and nowe I aduise thee hereafter to
expresse by thy doings, thy inward fayth, that God may be glorified, and turne no more to the puddle and vomit of your filthye
ydle life. And thus you see the long sufferance of God, and his pacience to vs warde, that he woulde haue no man to perishe, but
would all men come to repentance. And that you are now righteous, bee you more righteous still, and that you are holye, bee
you more holy still. &c. So that if these things be with you, and a-
bounde in you, they will make you (sayth S. Peter) that ye neuer
shal be ydle, nor vnfruitfull in the knowledge of our Lorde Iesus
Christ.

YOVTH. I perceyue now more and more still, how good and
profitable

Hierony.de
consec.dist.5
Cap Nunquã

Rom.6.4.
1.Thes.4.7
Iob.14.1.
Mar.13.35.
Rom.4.17.

Gal.5.10.
Mt.7.29.
Gal.1.23.
Prou.29.11.
2.Pet.3.22.
2.Pet.3.9.
Ezec.18.32.
Reue.22.11

2.Pet.18.

profitable it is, to accompany alwayes with the godlye, thereby a man shall learne godlynesse, for in the companie of the wicked, there is nothing but wickednesse to be learned.

Eccle.6.35.
Cap.8.9.
Cap.9.17.

A G E. It is good counsell (my sonne) that Salomon giueth, saying : Bring not euery man into thine house, for the deceytfull haue many traynes. &c. Againe he sayth : Who can be clensed by the vncleane ? For he that toucheth pitch, shall be defiled with it, and he that is familiar with the proude, shall be like vnto him. &c. according to the olde saying :

Eccl.11.27.
Cap.34.4.
Cap.13.1.

> If thou with him that haltes, doest dwell,
> To learne to halt, thou shalt full well.

YOVTH. By this your former discourse against ydlenesse, to haue men labour in their vocation and calling, doe you hereby include the lame, deafe, blinde, aged, impotent, sicke. &c. and suche as are not founde in their members. &c.

A G E. Nothing lesse. These are exempted, and therefore of necessitie must be holpen accordingly, with the ayde and comfort of the publike collection. Therfore he that giueth to the poore, lendeth to the Lorde, and what he layeth out, shall bee payde him againe. &c. The poore, sayth Christ, yee shall haue alwayes wyth you, and when ye will ye may doe them good. The fruite of the poore that is cast into their bosomes, wil returne again with great profit. Blessed is he that prouideth for the sick and nedy, the Lord shall deliuer him in the time of aduersitie. Giue almes (sayth Tobie) of thy substance, and turne not thy face from any poore, least God turne his face from thee. &c. Saint Paul willed the churches of the Corinthians, as he willed the churches of Galatia, to make gatherings euery first day of the weeke, and put aside and laye vp as God hath prospered them, that the necessitie of the saynts might be relieued. &c. Yet there must be a consideration in these also. For manye of them which lacke the vse of their feete, with their hands may pick wooll, and sow garments, or tose Okam. Many which lacke armes, may worke with their feete, to blowe Smithes bellowes. &c. to serue to go in errantes. &c. so as muche as maye bee

Prou.19.17.
Marc.14.7.
August.de
verbis dom.
Serm.26.
Psal.41.
Toby.4.
1.Cor.16.1.2
Act.11.29.
Rom 12.13.
Act.11.25.

in the respect of persons, we must labour to auoyde polenesse.

Herein also, we must consider to helpe the broken aged olde men and women, which neede to be susteyned of the common collection. Also those that be persecuted for the Gospell of Christe, *Math.25.35.* must be ayded likewise. Also captiues and prisoners, eyther at home, taken abrode in warres, or else with Turkes. Also menne that haue bene riche, & are fallen into pouertie, eyther by the seas, fire, or else by any other casualty, must likewise be holpe & succored. *Iames.1.27.* Also yong fatherlesse and motherlesse children, pore scholers, & neede-dy widowes. &c. & such other like, must be succoured, aided, and comforted, for the Church goodes are the goodes of the pore, and therfore you must not iudge, that I speake so vniuersallye, that these impotent and needy ought not to be holpen. &c. For as we reade in *Conc.Thuro. sub.Car.mag an.10. & 11.* Ludouicus the Emperors canonicall institutions, that *Res Ecclesiæ vota sunt fidelium, precia peccatorum, & patrimonia pauperum,* *In Instit. canonic sub. Ludouico Imp.an.830* The goodes of the church be the bowes and bequestes of the faithfull, prices to redeme them that are captiues and in prisons, and patrimonies to succour them with hospitalitie that be pore. Prosper also sayth: *Viros sanctos, res Ecclesiæ non vendicasse vt proprias: sed vt commendas pauperibus dimisse,* God men toke the goodes of *Prosp.in lib.1 de vita cont templ.cap.9.* the church, not as their owne, but distributed them, as giuen and bequeathed to the pore. Againe he sayth: *Quod habet, cum omnibus nihil habentibus habet commune,* Whatsoeuer the churche hath, it hath it in common, with all such as haue neede. It is reported that the churches did distribute these goods into foure parts: *Hebr.13.2.* one and the greatest part vpon the nedie people onely: the second parte for lodging of straungers: thirdlye, burying of the deade: fourthly, in healing of diseases. It is reported, that Serapion had *In tripart. hist.li.8.ca.1.* vnder him (*Decem millia sub se Monachorum, quos omnes sic educabat, vt ex proprijs sudoribus, necessaria compararet, & alijs ministraret egentibus*) Ten thousande Monkes, who brought them vp in such order, that they gate by their owne labours, sufficient for themselues, and also wherewithall to ayde and helpe the needye and indigent. &c. Nowe my sonne you perceyue what sorte of people I speake of, and what sort I speake not of.

YORTH.

YOVTH. You haue herein satisfied me fullye; I prayse God for it.

AGE. You doe well, to ascribe the prayse vnto God for it, for that euery good and perfect gift commeth from him. Iam.1.17.

YOVTH. Seing that we haue somewhat largely talked and reasoned togither of ydle playes and vaine pastimes, let me craue your further pacience, to knowe your iudgement and opinion as touching Playes and Players, which are commonlye vsed and much frequented in most places in these dayes, especiallye here in this noble and honourable citie of London.

AGE. You demaunde of me a harde question: if I should vtterly deny all kinde of such playes, then shoulde I bee thought too Stoicall & precise : If I allowe and admit them in generall, then shall I giue waye to a thousande mischiefes and inconueniences, which daily happen by occasion of beholding and haunting suche spectacles. Therfore let me vnderstande of what sort and kynde of Playes you speake of.

YOVTH. Are there manye kyndes and sortes of suche lyke Playes ?

AGE. Uerie many.

YOVTH. I pray you declare them vnto me, that I may learn what they are.

AGE. Some are called *Ludi Circenses,* whiche vsed to runne with chariots in the great compassed place in Rome called *Circus.* Others were called *Ludi Compatality,* which made Playes in the high wayes to the honour of Bacchus. Others were called *Ludi Florales,* which abhominable Playes in Rome; to the honour of their strumpetlike Goddesse *Flora,* in which cōmon women played naked, with wanton wordes and gestures. Another sorte were called *Ludi Gladiatory,* Games of Sworde players, fighting one with another in harnesse, in the sight of the people, endeuouring eche to kill other : a spectacle of crueltie to harden the peoples harts against killing in warres. Others are called *Ludi Gymnici,* exercises of running, leaping, throwing the darte, and wrastling. Others were called *Ludi Lupercales,* Games wherein yong Gentlemen.

Ludi Circenses.

Ludi compatalitij.

Ludi Florales.

Ludi Gladiatorij.

Ludi Gymnici.

Ludi Lupercales.

I.

men naked hauing whyppes in their handes, ranne about laughing and beating all that they mette. Another sorte were called

Ludi Mega
lenses.

Ludi Magalenses, Playes made to the honour of the mother
of the Goddes, with many and sundrie other such lyke vaine
Playes haue bene inuented.

YOVTH. I neuer hearde so much, nor so manye sortes of
Playes before, yet you haue not named those Playes & Players
which I woulde gladly heare of.

AGE. What Playes are they which you woulde so fayne
heare of?

YOVTH. They are Stage playes and Enterludes which are
nowe practised amongst vs so vniuersally in towne and country.

Histrix is a
little beast
vvith spec-
kled pric-
kles on his
back, vvhi-
che he vvil
cast of, and
hurt men ae
vvith them,
vvhich is
as Plinie
sayth, a
Porkepine.

AGE. Those are called *Histriones*, or rather *Histrices*, which
play vpon Scaffoldes and Stages, Enterludes and Comedies,
or otherwise with gestures. &c.

YOVTH. What say you to those Players and Playes? Are
they good and godly, meete to be vsed, haunted, and looked vppon
which nowe are practised?

AGE. To speake my minde and conscience plainly &(in the
feare of God) they are not tollerable nor sufferable in any common
weale, especially where the Gospell is preached. For it is right
prodigalitie, which is opposite to liberalitie. For as liberalitie is
to helpe and succour with worldly goods the man which is poore,
and standeth needefull thereof: and also to giue to the mariage of
poore Maydens, high wayes, or poore schollers, &c. So prodigalitie is to bestow mony and goods, in such sort as it spent, eyther
in banketting feasting, rewardes to players of Enterludes, Dicing, and Dauncing. &c. for the which no great fame or memory
can remayne to the spenders or receyuers thereof.

YOVTH. I haue hearde saye, that one Plautus a Comicall
Poet, spent all his substance vpon Players garments. Also one
Roscius a Romane and a player in Comedies (whom for hys
excellencie in pronunciation and gesture, noble Cicero called
his iewell) the Romaines also gaue him (as hystories reporte) a
stipende of one thousande groates for euery daye (which is in our
                                                         mony

mony rbj.li.riij.s.üij.d.) Lucius Silla being Dictatour, gaue
to him a ring of golde.&c. Sith these and such other gaue to such
vses, why may not we doe the like?

A G E. Bicause these are no examples for Christians to followe : for Christ hath giuen vs a farre better rule and order, how
to bestowe our goodes vpon his needie members whiche lie in the
streetes, prisons, and other places, and also those that are afflicted and persecuted for the testimonie of a good conscience for the
Gospels cause.&c. No man (sayth Chrysostome) was euer bla-
med, bicause he had not builded vp costly temples or churches.&c,
but euerlasting fire of hell (the punishment of the Deuilles) doe
hang ouer vs, except wee doe consider Christe in his members,
wandering as straungers, lacking harborough, and as prisoners
wanting visitation.&c. The like may I say of the giftes, buil-
dings, and maintenance of such places for Players , a spectacle
and schoole for all wickednesse and vice to be learned in. Saint
Augustine sayth : *Donare quippe res suas Histrionibus, vitium est
immane, non virtus,* Whosoeuer giue their goodes to Enterlude and Stage players, is a great vice and sinne, and not a vertue. What doe the hystories report of Plautus ende that was so
prodigall ?

YOVTH. I knowe not , therefore I praye you shewe
me.

A G E. Histories report, that he was brought into such pouertie, that he was fayne to serue a Baker in turning a Querne
or handmill to get his liuing.&c. Vespasian gaue out of his cof-
fers sire hundred pounde to Latine and Greeke readers . So did
Plinie his Nephewe the like, for the which they deserued greate
fame, and encreased in great welth and riches.

YOVTH. Doe you speake against those places also, whiche
are made vppe and builded for such Players and Enterludes , as
the *Theatre* and *Curtaine* is , and other suche lyke places besides?

A G E. Yea truly: For I am persuaded that Satan hath not
a more speedie way and fitter schoole to work and teach his desire,

Luc.12.23.
Math.19.23
Mar 14.7.
Mat.25
1.Tim.6.18

Chrisost.1.
tom.hom.54.

Aug. in Iohā.
tract.100.

Cooper

to bring men and women into his ſnare of concupiſcence and fil-thie luſtes of wicked whoredome, than thoſe places and playes, and theatres are : And therefore neceſſarie that thoſe places and Players ſhoulde be forbidden and diſſolued and put downe by authoritie, as the Brothell houſes and Stewes are . Howe did the Beniamites ouercome and take awaye the daughters of Iſ-racll ? but in watching them in a ſpeciall open place, where they were accuſtomed vppon the Feſtiuall dayes to ſporte and daunce moſt ydelly and wantonly. D. Peter Martyr (that famous learned man) vpon this place (ſayth:) Hereby we maye perceiue, that the virgins gaue themſelues to playes and daun-ces, which was to abuſe the feaſt day. It had bene better for thē to haue occupied themſelues about grauer matters. For the feaſt dayes were to this ende inſtituted, that the people ſhould aſſem-ble togither, to heare (not playes) but the worde of God, to bee preſent at the Sacrifices, where they ſhoulde both call vpon God, and communicate togither the Sacramentes inſtituted of God. Wherefore it is no maruayle if theſe Maidens were ſo ſtollen a-way, reſorting to ſuch open place. &c.

    Romulus (after that Remus his brother was ſlayne) erected and builded vp a certaine ſpectacle and place of ſafegarde for all tranſgreſſours that woulde come thither, practiſing thereby to rauiſhe all Maidens of the countrie reſorting to their newe ere-cted place in Mount Palatine, at ſolemne games and playes, o-uercame the people of Cenia, and ſlue their king. &c. Saint Au-guſtine ſayeth : That the women of Saba being of curioſitie deſirous to bee preſent at open ſpectacles, were rapted and ra-uiſhed by the Romaines : whereof followed ſuch warres, that both nations were almoſt deſtroyed. In conſideration of this and the like, Scipio Naſica (that worthie Romaine) obteyned in the Senate, that all Theatres and Stage playes ſhoulde be abolí-ſhed, for that it was ſo hurtfull vnto publike and ciuill maners. Alſo *s.c.* deſtroyed vtterlye that Theatre place, whiche was ſo gorgeouſly builded, and gaue commaundement; that no ſuche places ſhoulde be builded againe in the citie of Rome, and that they

they shoulde not make any seates or benches to sitte vpon (for to beholde such playes in suche places) neyther in the citie, nor yet within a myle compasse thereof. &c. I would to God our Magistrates would folow those good and wholesome examples.

YOVTH. I haue hearde manye both men and women saye, that they can resort to such playes, and beholde them without any hurt to themselues, or to others, and that no lust nor concupiscence is inflamed or stirred vp in them, in the beholding of anye person, or of the playes themselues. Howe say you, maye it be so?

A G E. Saint Chrysostome shall answere them, who wrote onely of such as you speake of, that resorted to such playing places. Some curious, daintie, and nyce persons (sayeth he) hearing this, will saye (to excuse their sinnes and follies) we that do resort to beholde and consider the beautie and fairenesse of women, at Theaters and Stage playes, are nothing hurt thereby. Dauid (sayeth he) was sore hurt (in beholding Bersabe) and thinkest thou to escape? He did not behold an harlot, but on the top of his house, *Tu autem in Theatro vbi condemnat animam sapientis,* Thou beholdest the in an open theatre, a place where ẏ soule of the wise is snared & condemned: in those places (sayth he) thou seest not only *Res infaustas,* vnlawfull things: but also hearest *spurciloquia,* filthie speaches, whereof is (sayth he) *incessu meretricis,* the beginning of whoredome, and the habite of all euilnesse and mischiefe, where thou shalt by hearing diuelishe and filthie songs hurte thy chaste eares, and also shalt see that which shall be greeuous vnto thine eyes: for our eyes are as windowes of the mynde, as the Prophete sayeth: Death entred into my windowes, that is, by mine eyes. Possible thou wilt say (sayeth he) I am not moued with those sightes. What art thou, yron (sayth he) stone, or an Adamant? art thou wiser, stronger, and holyer than Dauid? A little sparkle of fire cast into strawe, beginneth quickly to kindle & flame, our fleshe is strawe, and will burne quickly, and for that cause the holy ghost setteth Dauid for an example to vs, that we shoulde beware of such contagiousnesse. Job sayd: I haue

A good vvishe of the author.

Chrysost. in Psal. 50. hom. 1.

Prou. 7. 6. 7.

Ierem. 9. 1ø

Iam. 3. 5. 6. Prou. 6. 27.

Iob 31. 1.

I.iij.   made

made a couenant with mine eyes , why then shoulde I thinke vpon a Mayde ? Dauid also made his prayer to God, saying : O Lorde turne away mine eyes from regarding vanitie, and quicken me in thy way. Saint Ambrose vpon these wordes, calleth Stage playes, Uanitie, wishing that he coulde call backe the people which runne so fast thither , and willeth them to turne their eyes from beholding of such Playes and Enterludes. The lyke saying hath Saint Augustine.

Lactantius sayeth , that the eyes are diuers and variable, which are taken by the beholding of things, which are in the vse of men, nature, or delectable things. *Vitanda ergo spectacula omnia,* All suche spectacles and shewes (sayeth he) are therefore to bee auoyded, not onelye bicause vices shall not enter our heartes and breastes, but also least the custome of pleasure shoulde touche vs, and conuerte vs thereby both from God and good workes.

YOVTH. I perceyue by your communication, that none ought to haunt and frequente those Theatres and places where Enterludes are, and especially women and maydes.

AGE. You haue collected the meaning of my sayings (naye rather of the fathers sayings.) Truly you may see dayly what multitudes are gathered togither at those Playes, of all sortes, to the greate displeasure of almightie God , and daunger of their soules. &c. for that they learne nothing thereby, but that whiche is fleshlye and carnall. which Diogenes sawe and well perceyued, as appeared by his doings, when as vpon a certayne day he thrust himselfe into the Theatre or playing place, when as the people were comming forth. Being demaunded why hee did so, answered: bicause (sayth he) I will differ from the multitude, for the greatest parte of men are ledde rather by affections and reasons. &c. I wote not what precepts may be giuen our people, for our custome now is worse than it was amongst the Pagans. Therfore let the people, and especially women, giue eare to Pagan Ouid, if not to Christian preceptes, speaking of those common resortings vnto Playes, sayth :

The

They come to see, and eke for to be seene,
Full much chastitie quailed thereby hath beene.

Iuuenall the Poet sayeth also : That no wiues or maydens, that list to content and please sad and honest men, will be founde and seene at common Playes, Dauncings, or other great resorte of people. For these Playes be the instrumentes and armour of Uenus and Cupide, and to saye good soothe, what safegarde of chastitie can there be, where the woman is desired with so many eyes, where so many faces looke vpon hir, and againe she vpon so manye ? She must needes fire some, and hir selfe also fired againe, and she be not a stone : for what minde can bee pure and whole among such a rablement, and not spotted with any lust ? according to the olde Prouerbe, *Ex visu amor.* And as Uirgill sayth : *at vidi vt perij.&c.* Saint Cyprian persuadeth his friende Eucratius mightily, to leaue off, and not practise nor teach such Playes and Enterludes, shewing what inconueniences and wickednesse is gotten thereby, and what lust and concupiscence is stirred vp thereby in beholding of it, and what filthie and foule actes are done of whoredome and baudrie, to the hurte of the beholders, adding this, *Histrionicis gestibus inquinatur omnia,* By the gestures of Enterlude players, all honestie is defiled and defaced. Reade those places of S. Cyprian, which he wrote of purpose against Playes, for the inconueniences that hee sawe and hearde to come thereof. O Lorde what woulde he say & write of our playes nowe, if he were aliue and sawe their order in these dayes ?

Lodou. Viue

Cypria. libr.
Epist. 10. &
lib. 2. Epist. 2

For these causes was it, that the godly Fathers wrote so earnestly against such Playes and Enterludes, and also commaunded by Councels, that none shoulde go or come to Playes. As in the thirde Councel of Carthage, and in the Synode of Laodicea, It was decreed that no christians (and especially Priests) shoulde come into any place where Enterludes and Playes are, for that christians must abstain from such places where blasphemie is commonly vsed. Chrisostome calleth those places & playing of Enterludes, *Festa Satanæ,* Sathans banquets. Saluianus doth bitterly replie

Conc. 3. Cart
chag. cap. 11.
Syno. Laodi.
an. 368.
can. 54.

Chrysost. ho
sun Iob. 4

Saluianus in li.de prouid. dei.Fug.36.
repzehended thole men and women, that will not abſtaine from going to ſuch vaine Enterludes and Playes, ſaying: *Spernitur Dei templum, vt concurratur ad Theatrum: Ecclesia vacuatur, circus impletur: Chriſtum in altario dimittimus, vt adu lterantes viſu impuriſsimo oculos ludicorum turpium fornicatione paſcamus,* Hc deſpiſeth the Temple of God, that he maye runne to the Theatre: the Church is alwaye emptie and voyde, the playing place is repleniſhed and full: we leaue Chziſt alone at the aultar,and feede our eyes with vaine and vnhoneſt ſights, and with filthie and vncleane playes. And a little after, he declareth what innumerable vices there groweth by thoſe playes, and what ſinnes are committed againſt God and his lawes. &c. Alſo, Olympiodozus Olympiodor. in Eccleſuſt. cap.4. ſayth (to all Chziſtians,men and women in generall:) Abſtaine from pzophane ſpectacles and Enterludes, foz it is not meete that we ſhoulde go with thoſe feete vnto Playes,Enterludes, and abhominable ſpectacles,wherewith wee vſe to go into the Temple of God. Foz they that will go with cleane vnpolluted feete into the Church of God,muſt vtterly altogither abſtaine from vngodly and pzophane places, as theſe are.

YOVTH. Notwithſtanding all this that you haue alledged out of the Fathers and Counſelles, I ſuppoſe a man oz woman doth not ſinne to beholde and luſt one foz another,except they cōmit carnall copulation togither.

Math.5.28.
AGE. My ſonne, howe doeſt thou reade oz heare the wozds of Chziſt in the Goſpel,ÿ ſayth:He that looketh on a woman,and deſireth to haue hir, he hath cōmitted adulterie alredie in his heart, Rom.6.23. &c. And ſurely they are not ſpirituall, but carnall, which doe not beleeue that they haue a ſpzing of vngracionſneſſe within them, 1.Theſ.5.23 and foze not what the mynde be, but the bodie. I dare boldlye ſay, that fewe men oz women come from Playes and reſozts of men with ſafe and chaſte mindes . Therefoze Auguſtus Ceſar gaue cōmandement, that no woman ſhould come to ſee Wraſtlers and Players. The Maſſyliens (as Valerius ſayth) kepte ſo Henricus Cornelius Agrippa de van.ſcienſ. cap.20. great grauitie, that it woulde receyue into it no Stage players, bicau ſe the arguments (foz the moſte part) contayned the actes

and

and doings of harlots, to the ende that the custome of beholding such things, might not also cause a licence of following it : and therefore to exercise this arte, is not onely a dishonest and wicked occupation, but also to beholde it, and therein to delite, is a shamefull thing, bicause that the delite of a wanton mynde is an offence. &c. Alas my sonne, notwithstanding all this, are not almost all places in these our days replenished with Juglers, Scoffers, Feasters, and Players, which may saye and doe what they lyst, be it neuer so filthilye and fleshlye, and yet are suffered and hearde with laughing and clapping of handes. Lactantius saith: *Histrionum quoque impudicissimi motus, quid aliud nisi libidines docent, & instigant,* Those filthie and vnhonest gestures and mouings of Enterlude players, what other thing doe they teache, than wanton pleasure, and stirring vp of fleshly lustes vnlawfull appetites and desires ? With their bawdie and filthie sayings and counterseyt doings. Saint Paule therfore biddeth vs to abstaine from all appearance of euill. &c.

YOVTH. I maruayle why you do speake against such Enterludes and places for Players, seeing that many times they play histories out of the Scriptures.

AGE. Assuredly that is very euill so to doe, to mingle scurrilitie with Diuinitie, that is, to eate meate with vnwashed hands. Theopompus intermingled a portion of Moses lawe with his writings, for the which God strake him madde. Theodectes began the same practise, and was stricken starke blinde, and will God suffer them vnpunished, that with impure and wicked maners and doings, doe vse and handle vpon scaffolders, Gods diuine mysteries, with such vnreuerentnesse and irreligiousnesse? What fellowship hath righteousnesse with vnrighteousnes? what communion hath light with darknesse ? Out of one mouth (sayeth Saint James) proceedeth blessing and cursing, these things ought not so to be. S. Augustine sayth : It is better that spirituall things be vtterly omitted, than vnworthilye and vnreuerently handled and touched. O what rashnesse and madnesse is that (sayth Bernardes) to handle the worde of God with pollu-

K.   teth

(margin notes:) Alanus. / Rom.13. / Lacta. Firm. lib.6. ca.20. / Cypr. lib.2. 1 pist.2. / 1.Thes.5.22. / 2.Cor.5.14. / Iame.3.10.

ted handes, and to vtter and speake it with a filthie mouth, mingled with filthie speaches and wordes.

And by the long suffring and permitting of these vaine plays,
it hath stricken such a blinde zeale into the heartes of the people,
that they shame not to say and affirme openly, that Players are
as good as Sermons, and that they learne as much or more at a
Playe, than they doe at Gods worde preached. God be mercifull
to this Realme of Englande, for we begynne to haue ytching
eares, and lothe that heauenly Manna, as appeareth by their
slowe and negligent comming vnto Sermons, and running so
fast, and so many, continually vnto Playes. &c. Ouid was banished by Augustus into Pontus (as it is thought) for making
the booke of the Craft of Loue. Hiero Syracusanus did punishe
Epicharmus the Poet, bicause he rehearsed certaine wanton verses in the presence of his wife. For he woulde not haue onely in
his house chaste bodies, but also chaste eares. Why then shoulde
not Christians abolishe and punishe suche filthie Players of
Enterludes, whose mouthes are full of filthinesse and wickednesse. Saint Paule willed the Ephesians, that fornication and
all vncleannesse shoulde not once be named among them. Neyther filthinesse, neyther foolishe talking, neyther iesting, whiche
are things not comely: but rather giuing of thankes. He sheweth the reason to the Corinthians why they shoulde so abstayne:
Bicause euill speakings corrupt good maners (sayth he.) Again:
Come out from among them, and let vs seperate our selues, and
touche no vncleane thing, and then the Lorde will receyue vs,
and abide with vs. For (sayth he) the grace of God that bringeth
saluation vnto all men, hath appeared, and teacheth vs, that we
shoulde deny vngodlynesse and worldly lusts, and that we shoulde
liue soberly, righteously, and godlily in this present worlde, looking for the blessed hope and appearing of the glorie of the mightie God, and of our sauiour Iesus Christ.

YOVTH. Nowe I perceyue it is not good nor godly haunting of such places.

AGE. It is truth. For as the Preacher sayth: It is better

Margin notes:
1.Tim.4.3.
Num.11.4.
5.6.7.

Hiero Syra-
cusanus.

Ephes.5.4.

5.

2.Cor.15.33
2.Cor.6.17

Tit.2.11.12

13.

Ecclef.7.4.

to

to go vnto the house of mourning, than go to the house of feasting. &c. For the heart of the wise is in the house of mourning:
but the heart of fooles is in the house of myrth. And therefore it
is better (sayth Salomon) to heare the rebuke of a wise man, than
that a man should heare the songs of fooles.

YOVTH. Truly I see many of great countenance both men
and women resort thither.

AGE. The more is the pittie, and greater is their shame
and payne, if they repent not, and leaue it off. Many can tarie
at a vayne Playe two or three houres, when as they will not a-
byde scarce one houre at a Sermon. They will runne to euerye
Playe, but scarce will come to a preached Sermon, so muche
and so great is our follye, to delyte in vanitie, and leaue veritie,
to seeke for the meate that shall perishe, and passe not for the
foode that they shall liue by for euer. These people sayeth Iob,
haue their houses peaceable, without feare, and the rod of God is
not vpon them, they sende forth their children like sheepe, and
their sonnes daunce. They take the Tabret and Harpe, and reioyce in the sounde of Instruments. They spende their dayes in
welth, & sodenly they go down to the graue. They say vnto God,
depart from vs. For we desire not the knowledge of thy wayes.
Who is the almightie that we shoulde serue him? and what profite shoulde wee haue, if we shoulde pray to him? Therefore I
speake (alas with griefe and sorowe of heart) against those people that are so fleshlye ledde, to see what rewarde there is giuen
to suche Crocodiles, whiche deuoure the pure chastitie, bothe
of single and maried persons, men and women, when as in
their Playes you shall learne all things that appertayne to
crafte, mischiefe, deceptes, and filthinesse. &c. If you will learne
howe to bee false, and deceyue your husbandes, or husbandes
their wyues, howe to playe the harlottes, to obtayne ones
loue, howe to rauishe, howe to beguyle, howe to betraye,
to flatter, lye, sweare, forsweare, howe to allure to whoredome, howe to murther, howe to poyson, howe to disobey

Iob.21.2.
6.
7.
11.
12.
13.
14.
15.

and

and rebell agaynſt Princes, to conſume treaſures prodigally, to mooue to luſts, to ranſacke and ſpoyle cities and townes, to bee ydle, to blaſpheme, to ſing filthie ſongs of loue, to ſpeake filthily, to be prowde, howe to mocke, ſcoffe, and deryde any nation, lyke vnto Geneſius Aralatenſis. &c. ſhall not you learne then at ſuche Enterludes howe to practiſe them ? as Palingenius ſayth :

Geneſius Aralatenſis patria, vvas a common Ieaster and Player to Domitian the Emperor, vvhich did mocke and ſcoffe most filthily vvith his ieſtures, the godly chriſtians. &c.

> *Index eſt animi ſermo morúmꝗ́ fidelis,*
> *Haud dubiè teſtu.*

The tongue hath oftentimes witneſſe brought,
Of that which heart within hath thought :
And maners hidde in ſecret place,
It doth diſcloſe and oft diſgrace.

Therefore great reaſon it is that women (eſpeciallye) ſhoulde abſent themſelues from ſuch Playes. What was the cauſe why Dina was rauiſhed ? was it not hir curioſitie ? the Mayden woulde go forth , and vnderſtande the maners of other folkes. Curioſitie then no doubt did hurt hir, and will alwayes hurt women. For if it were hurtfull vnto the familie of Iacob (being ſo great a Patriarch) for a Mayden to wander abroade, how much more daungerous is it for other families, which are not ſo holye nor acceptable vnto God ? But the nature of women is muche infected with this vice. And therefore Saint Paule admoniſheth women to loue their huſbands, to bring vp their childzen, and to be byders and tariers at home. And when he entreateth of wanton and yong widdowes : They wander abroade (ſayth he) and runne from houſe to houſe, and at the laſt go after Satan. Giue the water no paſſage, no not a little (ſayth Syrach) neyther giue a wanton woman libertie to go out abroade. If thy daughter be not ſhamefaſt, holde hir ſtraitly, leaſt ſhe abuſe hir ſelfe thorow ouermuch libertie. As men cannot gather grapes of thornes, and figges of thiſtles, neyther can anye man or woman gather anye vertue or honeſtie in haunting places where Enterludes are . As one vertue bringeth in another, ſo one vice nouriſheth another.

Gene.34.1.

Titus.2.4.
Epheſ.5.23.

Timo.5.13.

Eccl.25.27.

Math.7.16.

Pryde

Pryde ingendzeth enuie : and ydlenesse is an entraunce into lust.
Jdlenesse is the myſtreſſe of wanton appetites, and poztreſſe of
Luſts gate. Foz no mã entreth into the pallace of Luſt, vnleſſe he
be firſt let in by Jdleneſſe, and moze Jdleneſſe can there not bee,
than where ſuch Playes and Enterludes are. Therfoze as Chzift *Math.6.22*
ſayth : The light of the bodie is the eye : If then the eye be ſingle,
thy whole bodie ſhall be light. But if thine eye bee wicked, then
all thy body ſhall be darke. &c. Is if he would ſaye : If thine affections and wicked concupiſcence ouercõme reaſon, it is no mar-
uell though men be blinded and be lyke vnto beaſtes, and followe
all carnall pleaſures. To take away this darkeneſſe and blinde- *Athenians.*
neſſe, the Athenians prouided well when they appoynted their
Areopagites to wzite no Comedie oz Play, foz that they woulde
auoyde all euils that might enſue thereof. &c. Theodoſius like- *Theodoſius.*
wiſe did by expreſſe lawes decree that daunces and wanton dali-
ance ſhoulde not be vſed, neyth'r Games oz Enterludes. Con- *Conſtantinus*
ſtantinus the Emperour made lawes, wherein he did vtterly foz- *centur.4.*
bidde all Enterludes and ſpectacles among the Romanes, foz the *cap.3.fo.76.*
great diſcommoditie that came thereof.

Saint Cypzian ſayth, it is not ynough foz his frende Eucra- *Cypria.lib.1*
tius to abſtayne from ſuch Enterlude Playes himſelfe, but alſo *Epiſt.10.*
he muſt not teach others, noz encourage them thereto . S. Im- *Ambr.lib.1*
bzoſe ſayth : that all ſuch Playes (though they ſeeme pleaſant and *offic.cap.23.*
full of ſpozt) muſt vtterly be aboliſhed, bicauſe no ſuch Playes are
mentioned noz expreſſed in holy Scripture. S. Auguſtine ſayth : *Auguſt.lib.1*
that ſuch Enterludes and Playes are filthie ſpectacles. Foz when *cap.32.de*
the Heathen did appoint and ozdeyne (ſayth he) Playes and En- *ciuitate dei*
terludes to their Gods, foz the auoyding of the Peſtilence of their
bodies : your Biſhops foz the auoyding of the peſtilence of your
ſoules, hath prohibited and forbidden thoſe kynde of Scenicall
and Enterlude playes. Thus yon may perceiue and vnderſtande
howe thoſe Playes haue bene thought off among the good and
godly Fathers afoze time, which inſtructe vs thereby to hate and
deteſt the like now in this latter time practiſed.

YOVTH. Is there no lawes oz decrees that haue bene made

against such players of Enterludes, sith they are so noysome & pestilence to infect a Common wealth?

A. G. E. Uery many lawes and decrees.

YOVTH. I pray you expresse some of them for the better satisfying of my minde herein.

A. G. E. I will so doe God willing. It was decreed vnder

Conc. Arelatsensis. 2. 20.

Constantinus the Emperour, that all Players of Enterludes shoulde be excluded from the Lordes table. Johannes de Burgo sometime Chauncelour of Cambridge, and a Doctor of Diuinitie, in his booke entituled *Pupilla oculi,* sayeth, that *Histriones,* Enterlude players, *Non sunt ad ordines promouendi,* are not to be promoted to any dignitie, the reason is (sayth he) *Quia sunt infames,* for that those Players are infamous persons. He noteth further howe they are knowen, *Hoc intellige de his quibus qui publicè coram populo faciunt aspectum siue ludibrium sui corporis exercendo opus illud,* Understande this of those Players whiche vse to make shewes openly before the people, or else in vsing their, bodies to this businesse, as to make sport to be laughed at. In another place he sayth: *Histrionibus, Magicis, Scenicis, & alijs infamibus notorijs & manifestis, non est Eucharistia conferenda, quia tales vitâ ducunt illicitam,* The Sacrament of thanksgiuing ought not to be ministred vnto stage players of Enterludes, or to Witches, Sorcerers, or to anye suche infamous and notorious wicked persons, for that they leade a lewde and vngodly lyfe. In the decrees, it is so decreed, that all Enterlude players, and Comedie players, Heretikes, Jewes, and Pagans, are infamous persons, and ought to be taken for no accusers of any, nor yet to bee produced as witnesses in any matter or cause before any Judge, if they be the law is, that the partie may lawfully except against them, & say, they are infamous persons, for they are Players of Enterludes. And this may you doe also against common Minstrels. S. Augustine sayth also, that those Enterlude players are infamous persons. Cornelius Agrippa sayeth: There was in times past no name more infamous than Stage players. And all they that hadde played an Enterlude in the Theatre, were by the

Ioh de Burg.
in pupilla o-
culi, 7.pars
sis, cap. 50.
Distinct. 33.
cap. Marini.

Pupilla oculi
quart. partis.
Cap. 8. I.
Distinct. 86.
Cap. Donare.

Summa An-
gelica.

Causâ. 4.
quest. 1. c. 1. 1.
Distinc. 2. de
consecr. cap.
pro dilectio-
ne.
§ De his qui
no. infr. s. l. ij.
* a's pretor
vlt.
Aug. lib. 1. 2
cap. 14. de
ciuitate dei.
H. Cornelius
Agrippa de
vanit. scien.
cap. 20.

the Lawes depriued from all honoure and dignitie. Also there is a notable Statute made againste Uagabondes, Roges.&c. wherein is expressed what they are that shall bee taken and accounted for Roges. Amongst all the whole rablement, Common players in Enterludes are to be taken for Roges, and punishment is appoynted for them to bee burnte through the eare with an hote yron of an ynche compasse, and for the second fault to be hanged as a Felon.&c. The reason is, for that their trade is such an ydle loytering life, a practise to all mischiefe, as you haue hearde before.

An. Elizab. 14.cap.5.

YOVTH. If they leaue this lyfe, and become good true labourers in the Common wealth, to gette their owne liuings with their owne handes, in the sweate of their face, shall not they be admitted and taken againe to the Lords table, and afterwarde to be reputed and taken for honest men?

AGE. Yes trulye. And therefore in the thirde Councell of Carthage, it is put downe in these wordes: *Scenicis atque Histrionibus, cæterísq́ personis huiusmodi, vel Apostatis, conuersis ad Dominum, gratia vel reconciliatio non negetur,* To Players of Enterludes and Comedies, and other such lyke infamous persons and Apostates, conuerting and returning to the Lorde (by repentance) grace and reconciliation is not to bee denyed. And this is according to the saying of the Prophete Ezechiell: If the wicked will returne from all his sinnes that he hath committed, & kepe all my statutes, and doe that which is lawfull and right, he shall surely liue and not die.&c.

Concilium 3. Carthagine. cap.35. De consecra. Dist.2.cap. Scenicis ate que histriovi nibus.

Ezec.18.21.

YOVTH. I pray you shewe mee from whence this kinde of Playes had their beginning, and who deuised them.

AGE. Chrysostome sayth: the Deuill founde oute Stage playes first, and were inuented by his craste and policie, for that they conteyne the wicked astes and whoredomes of the Goddes, whereby the consciences of godly men are grieuously wounded, and wicked lustes are many wayes stirred vp. And therefore the Diuell builded Stages in cities.

Chrisost. in Mat.hom.6.

Arnobius sayeth: The Heathens supposed to haue pleased

Arnobius lib.7.

and

and pacified their Gods from their wrath and displeasure, when as they dedicated to them the sounds of Instruments and Shalmes. &c. Stage playes and Enterludes. Saint Augustine sayth: The heathen did appoint Playes and Enterludes to their Gods, for the auoyding of pestilent infections. &c. Theophylus sayth : *Gentes suos dies habebant quibus publica spectacula. & c. religiosa. &c.* The Gentyles had their certaine dayes appointed for open spectacles and shewes &c. which they dedicated religiouslye vnto their Gods. Clemens and others say : *Diabolus sit author Gentilium superstitionum,* That the Deuil is the author of the Gentiles superstitions. For these causes & many other, sayth Theophilus, christians were forbidden to vse any such like Playes. &c. If you will know more hereof, I will referre you vnto Polydore Virgil, and also vnto John Textor, where you shall fully see the originall of all those Playes. &c.

YOVTH. I maruaile much (this being as you say) that these Playes and Enterludes are tollerated and suffered nowe a dayes in a Common wealth, being so euill of it selfe, and hauing so euill patrons.

AGE. It is much to be maruayled at in dede, my sonne, for where Gods Gospell is preached and taught, such vaine vyle and filthie pastimes should surcease, and be banished far away from Christians, from whence it came. Beatus Rhenanus sayth : *Non solum temperandum fuit, qua manifestam prae se ferrent impietatem : sed, etiam. &c.* It was meete for them to refrayne, not onely from such things, as haue a manifest shew of wickednesse, but also from such things as might bee called indifferent, partly least anye of the weaker christians should be corrupted : partly also, least the heathens should be encouraged in their errors, thinking that thing, for that the christians themselues dee it, to be the better. Tertullian sayth also : *De hoc primo consiliam. &c.* Herein will I first stande, whether it be lawfull for the seruant of God, to communicate with whole nations in such things : eyther in apparell, or in diet. or in anye other kynde of their pastimes and mirth. Saint Basill sayth : *Let ydlenesse and super-*

fluous

August. lib. 2 cap. 32. de ciuitate dei.

Theoph. lib. 3 contra Aus tolicum.

Clem. in oratione ad gentes. Theoph. lib. 2 cont. Auтol. Tatianus in orat. contra Graecos.

Pol. Virgil. de rerum inuēt lib. 3. cap. 3. Io. Rauisi Textoris officina fo. 906

B. Rhenanus in librum de corona milit.

Tertul. de Idolatria.

Basil. de nat ali. Chri. li.

fluous things bee put to silence, where Gods churche is. What meaneth this (sayth Saint Origen) leaue hir no maner of remnant. The meaning is this: Abolishe not certaine of the superstitions of the Chaldes, reseruing certaine. Therefore he commaundeth that nothing be left in hir, be it neuer so little. Therefore S. Augustine sayth, that his mother left bringing of wine and cakes to the church, for that she was warned, it was a resemblance of the superstition of the heathen. Tertullian reasoneth vehemently, that a christian man ought not to go with a Laurell garland vpon his heade, and that for none other cause, but onely for that the Heathens vsed so to go. &c. How much more should we leaue off to imitate those filthie Playes and Enterludes that came from the Heathens, nay from the Deuill himselfe. But as one sayth: *Dolosi hominis dolosa vestis,* Craftie man, craftie coate. These Players, as Seneca sayth: *Malunt personam habere quàm faciem,* They will rather weare a visarde, than a naturall face. And therefore Saint Cyprian vehemently inueygheth againste those which contrarie to nature and the lawe doe attire themselues being men, in womens apparell, and women in mennes apparell, with Swannes fethers on their heads, Silkes, and golden apparell, &c. shewing forth in their Playes very Uenus it self, as if they were fully in the kingdome of Sathan. &c.

YOVTH. You haue, in my iudgement, paynted oute those things to the full, and opened suche matters by the effectes, as will lothe any honest man or good woman to come neare suche Playes.

AGE. Nay truly, I haue rather giuen but an ynkling hereof, than opened the particular secrets of the matter.

YOVTH. The publishing and opening of the filthie matters thereof, is sufficient to proue that they ought to be ouerthrowne and put downe.

AGE. You say truth.

YOVTH. Yet I see little sayd and lesse done vnto them, great resort there is daily vnto them, and thereout sucke they no small aduauntage.

Origen in Iere.hom.3.

Aug.cont fauſt.li.6.ca.2

Tertul.de coron.militis.

Le.18.3.30.

Macrobius.

Seneca.

Cypria.lib.1. Epiſt.10. Lib.2.Epiſt.2e.

Deu.22.5.

B. Alanus

A G E. They are like vnto the citizens of Sybaris, whiche were in all kinde of sensualitie delicious, farre passing all other, for they vsed commonly to bidde their guestes a whole yeare before, that neyther the bidder might lacke time to prepare all dainties, and delicious fare, and costly furniture, nor the guestes to adorne and trimme themselues vp with golde, &c. So they vse to set vp their billes vpon postes certaine dayes before, to admonishe the people to make their resort vnto their Theatres, that they may thereby be the better furnished, and the people prepared to fill their purses with their treasures, that they maye sing, which Horace sayth :

Hor. lib. 1
Epist.

> Nowe are the braue and golden dayes,
> Nowe fame with play we gayne,
> And golde can shewe vs many wayes
> Mens fauour to attaine :
> For mony they heare the Musicke sweete,
> And Playes they buye with golde,
> We seeke for golde, and straight vnmeete,
> Our name by it is solde.

Therefore of them Boetius sayth :

> Howe they doe get, fewe folkes doe care,
>   but riches haue they must,
> By hooke or crooke we dayly see,
>   they drawe men to their lust.

Idem.

> No faith nor feare of God haue they,
>   which doe those playes pursue :
> Their hands are giuen to sell and spoyle,
>   their gaine they call their due.

YOVTH. I doe nowe well perceyue the wickednesse hereof, by that I haue hearde of you, out of auncient authorities, Councels, Lawes, and Decrees, and I woulde to God suche lawes were nowe executed vpon such things, which are occasions and loade
stones

ſtones to draw people to wickednes. J maruaile the magiſtrates
ſuffer them thus to continue, and to haue houſes builded for ſuch
exerciſes and purpoſes which offend God ſo highly, ſithe it came
fom the Heathen, Sathan being the author, as you haue proued: For my part J ſhall henceforth (Jeſus Chriſt willing) abſent my ſelfe from ſuch places and theatres, and ſhall prouoke o-
thers to doe the like alſo. &c. Yet J maruayle much, ſithe the rulers are not onely negligent and ſlowe herein to doe, but the
Preachers are as dumme to ſpeake and ſaye in a Pulpitte a-
gaynſt it.

AGE. J doubt not but God will ſo moue the hearts of Magiſtrates, and looſe the tongue of the Preachers in ſuch godly ſort
(by the good deuout prayers of the faithfull) that both with the
ſworde and the worde, ſuch vnfruitfull and barren trees ſhall be
cut downe, to Gods great glorie, comfort and ſafetie of his people, and encreaſe of vertue and chriſtianitie, whiche God graunt
for his Chriſt Jeſus ſake.

Auguſt.io Pſalm.81.

YOVTH. Amen, Amen, good Lorde.

AGE. Nowe that you are reſolued in this poynt, according
vnto your requeſt and deſire, let this ſuffice at this time, as touching this matter, and let vs go forwarde to reaſon of ſome o-
ther matter.

YOVTH. Before we reaſon of anye other matter, lette me
vnderſtande your iudgement as touching Comedies, and ſuche
lyke things, whiche Schollers doe manye times practiſe and
vſe, both in the Vniuerſities, and alſo in diuerſe other good
Schooles.

AGE. Saint Cyprian wryting vnto his friende Euagri-
us in a certaine Epiſtle, ſayth that he is (*Doctor non erudiendo-*
rum, ſed perdendorum puerorum, &c.) A teacher not of learning, but of deſtroying childre, which practiſe them in theſe Enterlude and Stage playes. For (ſayth he) *Quod malè didicit, cæteris*
quoq; inſinuat: that euil which he hath learned, he doth alſo communicate vnto others. &c. Notwithſtanding, you ſhall vnderſtand ŷ
S. Cyprian ſpeaketh here of him that did teach and practiſe only

Cypr. Epiſt 10 libr.4

this kynde of baine pastimes and playes, and did allure children vp therein. But to shewe you my minde plainlye, I thinke it is lawfull for a Scholemaister to practise his schollers to play Comedies, obseruing these and the like cautions. First that those Comedies which they shall play, be not mixt with any ribaudrie and filthie termes and wordes (which corrupt good manners.) Secondly, that it be for learning and vtterance sake, in Latine, and very seldome in Englishe. Thirdly, that they vse not to play commonly, and often, but verye rare and seldome. Fourthlye, that they be not prankced and decked vp in gorgious and sumptuous apparell in their play. Fiftly, that it be not made a common exercise publikely for profit and gaine of mony, but for learning and exercise sake. And lastly, that their Comedies bee not mixte with baine and wanton toyes of loue. These being obserued, I iudge it tollerable for schollers.

YOVTH. What difference is there, I pray you, betwene a Tragedie and a Comedie?

AGE. There is this difference: A Tragedie properly is that kinde of Play, in the which, calamities and miserable endes of Kings, Princes, and great Rulers are described and sette forth, and it hath for the most part a sadde and heauy beginning and ending. A Comedie hath in it, humble and priuate persons, it beginneth with turbulent and troublesome matters, but it hath a merie ende.

¶ An Inuectiue against Dice playing.

With you haue instructed me so well against Idlenesse, and baine Pastimes, and Playes, I pray you instruct mee further also, as touching other playes (especially of one kinde of playe) which is commonly vsed of most people in this land, whether it be euill or good to be vsed?

AGE.

1. Cor. 15. 33.

A G E. According vnto my simple talent, I shall be readie to imploye it, in what I may, for your better instruction, and therfore declare vnto me among all, what playe that is which you meane, which you say is so much practised now a dayes amongst all sortes and degrees.

YOVTH. If you will giue mee a walke or two aboute the fields, I will declare the whole matter of the play, for I woulde gladly heare your iudgement of it.

A G E. I will go with you willingly, and heare your talke gladly, and wherein I maye doe you any good, I shall be readie (the Lorde willing) to satisfie your request, whiche is my desire.

YOVTH. Sir, I preise you humble duetie for this your so great and vndeserued curtesie, come on, leade you the waye, good father, I beseech you, for reuerence is due vnto the aged, as Moses sayth : Rise vp before the hore heade, and honour the person of the aged.

Leui.19.52.
Pro.20.29.

A G E. The honourable age (sayeth Salomon) is not that which is of long time, neyther that whiche is measured by the number of yeares : but wisedome (sayth he) is the gray heare, and an vndefiled life is the old age. Nowe my sonne, say on in Gods name what you haue to say.

Wis.4.8.

9.

YOVTH. In our former communication betweene vs, you haue spoken against vaine Playes and ydle Pastimes, yet you allowed of certaine moderate and actiue pastimes, for exercise and recreations sake.

A G E. It is very true, I graunted it, and doe allow of them, so farre forth as they are vsed to that ende wherefore they were appointed.

YOVTH. I pray you let me vnderstande what those Playes are, which you allowe off, and also of those which you allowe not off.

A G E. Before I speake of them, it shall be good to distribute and deuide Playes into their formes and kindes.

YOVTH. I pray you doe so.

A G E. I must herein make two exceptions: First is, that by this my speach I meane not to condemne such publike games or prices as are appoynted by the Magistrate: Secondly, that such games as may benefite (if neede require) the Common wealth are tollerable.

YOVTH. I pray you let me heare your diuision of Playes in their kyndes.

A G E. There are some kinde of Playes which are vtterly referred vnto chaunce, as he whiche casteth moste, or casteth thys chaunce or that (at Dice (carieth away the rewarde. There are other, wherby the powers either of the body or mind are exercised.

YOVTH. I pray you speake first of those Playes, which are for the exercise of the bodie and minde.

A G E. Those Playes which are for the exercise eyther of the powers of mynde or bodie, are not vtterly forbidden. Iustinian when he had vtterly taken away Playes that depended of chance (at Dice) ordeyned certaine kinde of Playes, as throwing a round ball into the ayre (which play is at this day much vsed among my countrimen of Deuonshire) handling and tossing the Pyke or staffe, running at a marke, or such like. &c. Aristotle in his Rhetorikes, commendeth these exercises of the bodie. So we see at this daye, publike wealthes do sometime set forth vnto such as can best vse weapons, a reward or price, to the ende they may haue the people the better encouraged and exercised (alwayes taking heede, that these Playes be not hurtfull or pernitious, and that it be not daungerous, eyther to themselues, or to the beholders, as are the Turneys, and such like. &c. Such kinde of playes are forbidden, *Ad legem Aquiliam,* in the Lawe, *Nam Ludus,* and in the Decretals, it is also expressed, *De tornementis.*

YOVTH. What other Playes are there which are tollerable?

A G E. That which was vsed of olde time.

YOVTH. What Playes were that I beseech you?

A G E. To labour with poyses of Leade, or other mettall, called in Latine, *Alteres.* Lifting and throwing of the stone, barre, or bowle with hande or foote, casting of the darte, wrast-

ling,

Iustinian

Decret. lib. 5 in gloss. cap. ludorū.

ling, shooting in long Bowes, Crossebowes, Handgunnes, ryding, trayning vp men in the knowledge of martiall and warrelike affaires and exercises, knowledge to handle weapons, to leap and vault, running, swimming, Barriers, running of horses, at the tilt, or otherwise, which are called in Latine, *Luda, Discus, Cursus, siue Saltus. Cestus, Certamen equestre vel Currule.* All which Playes are recited partly by Homer, partly by Vergil, and partly by Pausanias. &c.

Hom. lib.3.
Vergil.lib.5.
Eneid.

YOPT H. What say you by hauking, hunting, and playing at Tennise?

A. G. E. These exercises are good, and haue bene vsed in ancient times, as we may reade in Genesis. Cicero sayth: *Suppeditant autem & campus noster, & studia venandi, honesti exempla ludendi,* The fieldes (sayth he) hunting of beastes and such other, doe minister vnto vs goodly occasions of passing the time, yet he addeth thereunto this saying: *Ludendi est quidem modus retinendus,* A measure ought to be kept in pastime. For in these dayes many Gentlemen will doe (almost) nothing else, or at the least, can doe that better than any other thing. And this is the cause why there are found so many raw captaines & souldiers in Englande, among our Gentlemen, when time of seruice requireth. And also it is the cause of so many vnlearned Gentlemen as there are. For they suppose that it is no part belonging to their calling, for to heare sermons, pray, and studie for learning, nor to be exercised in heroicall actes and martiall affaires, but onely to hauke and hunt all day long.

Gene.27.5.
Cicero.

YOVTH. I haue hearde olde woodmen saye, hee cannot be a Gentleman which loueth not a dogge.

A G E. If that be true, he cannot be a dog that loueth not a Gentleman. As I doe not hereby condemne all Gentlemen, so must I nedes (God be praysed) iustifie many, which are desirous to heare preaching, to vse praier, study for lerning, & exercise martiall affaires, readie to serue at al commandements for iust causes.

YOVTH. What say you to Musicke and playing vpon Instruments, is not that a good exercise?

A G E.

A G E. Musicke is very good, if it be lawfully vsed, and not vnlawfully abused, therefore I thinke good first to declare, from whence it had his beginning, and to what end it was instituted. Secondly, whether they may be kept in the Churches. Lastly, what kinde of songs and measures are profitable and healthfull.

Y O V T H. I beseech you let me heare this throughly, and I will giue attentiue eare therevnto, for that some men dispraise it to much, and thinke it vnlawfull, others commende it as much, and thinke nothing so lawfull : and a thirde sort there are, which make it a thing indifferent.

A G E. Two sorts that you speake of, are to be reproued, but the thirde sorte is to be commended.

Y O V T H. I praye you let me heare your iudgement hereof, and first of all, as you promised, of the beginning and institution thereof.

A G E. As touching the first : Men of the olde time were accustomed with common vowes to sing certaine solemne ditties, both when they gaue thankes to God, and also when as they woulde obteyne any thing of him. Wherefore Orpheus, Limus, Pindarus, and Horace, and suche like Poetes, which vsed the Harpe, wrote their hymnes for the most part, for these vses. Also in the Romane publike wealth, the Priests of Mars which were called *Salij,* caried shieldes, and sang their verses through the citie. Furthermore it was the manner, that Musicke and verses were had, when the prayses of noble men were celebrated, chiefly at feastes, whereby they which stode by, might be admonished, to imitate their noble actes, and detest suche vices, which were cōtrarie vnto their vertues. Moreouer, they vsed them to recreate the mindes, and to comfort such as were pensiue, heauy, and sad for the deade. As Saule being heauie. &c. caused Dauid to playe vpon the Harpe to refresh him &c. The vse hereof also we maye reade in Mathewe, when as Christ our Sauiour came into the Rulers house to raise vp his deade daughter, the Minstrels and people were making a noyse, that is (according to their custome) to play and sing. &c. Contrariwise, when any great cause of ioye happened,

Sabij.
1 Sam 16. 23
Math. 9. 23.
Exo 15. 120

happened, it was expressed by Musicke and songs, as wee maye reade many examples hereof in the holy Scriptures, as of Moyses sister Miriam, Judith, Jephtah his daughter. &c. Likewise in weddings they were wont to playe musically, and to sing wedding songs. All these things if they bee done moderately, and in due time, are tollerable. For Musicke and songs containe three kindes of good things, that is, honest, profite, and pleasantnesse. For although singing of it selfe delighteth the mindes of men, yet when wordes are ioyned vnto it, which are of a iust number, and bounde by certaine feete (as Verses are) is much more pleasant. And vndoubtedly Poetrie had hereof his beginning, and cannot be denied but it is an excellent gift of God: yet this ought to bee kept pure and chast among men, bicause certaine lasciuious men haue and doe filthily defile it, applying it to wantonnesse, wicked lusts, and euery filthie thing.

Iudg. 11.34.
Iudet. 16.2.

YOVTH. Why doth Musicke so rapte and rauishe men in a maner wholy?

AGE. The reason is playne. For there are certaine pleasures, which onely fill the outwarde senses: and there are others also, which pertaine only to the mynde or reason. But Musick is a delectation so put in the middest, that both by the sweetenesse of the soundes it moueth the senses, and by the artificiousnesse of the number and proportions, it deliteth reason it selfe. And that happeneth then chiefly, when such wordes are added vnto it, whose sense is both excellent and learned. Pithagoras opinion was, that they which studied his doctrine, shoulde be brought in sleepe with a harpe, and by the accordes thereof also wakened, whereby they might quietly enioy the time both of sleeping and waking. Cicero affirmeth, that rockes and wildernesses doe giue a sounde, and cruell beasts by singing are assuaged, and made to stande still, as it is reported of the Vnicorne: when as men will take him, they put a yong mayden into the wildernesse, and when the Vnicorne seeth hir, he standeth still, and when hee heareth the mayde sing and play on an instrument, he commeth to hir, and sleepeth harde by hir, and layth his head vpon hir lap, and so the hunters kill him.

Pythagoras

Cicero.

M.   I

I may also speake howe the Poetes fable, that when the walles of Thebes the citie were buylt, the stones of their owne motion came togither with the sounde of the Harpe. And no man is ignorant, what the same Poetes haue written of Arion (who being taken by pyrates) playing so melodiously vppon his harpe, the Dolphin fishe, with the great Whales, delyted so muche in his Musicke, that when as the Pyrates cast him into the sea, the fishes caried him safely vnto the shore. So haue they fayned of

Orpheus. And also who knoweth not howe muche Dauid here and there in his Psalmes, prayseth bothe Musicke and Songs.

Secondly, we must consider whether it may be vsed in Churches. In the East part the holy assemblies euen from the beginning, vsed singing, which we maye easily vnderstande by the testimonie of Plinie in his Epistle to Traiane the Emperour:

where he writeth that Christians vsed to sing hymnes before day vnto their Christ, and therefore were called *Antelucanus cœtus*, the morning assemblies. And this is not to bee ouerslipte, that these wordes were written in that time that Iohn the Euange-

list liued, for he was aliue vnto the time of Traian. Wherefore if a man shall saye, that in the time of the Apostles there was singing in holy assemblies, he shall not stray from the truth. Paule

who was before these tymes, vnto the Ephesians, sayth: Be not drunke with wine, wherein is excesse: but be filled with the spirite, speaking vnto your selues in Psalmes and Hymnes, and spirituall songs, singing and making melodie to the Lorde in your hearts, giuing thankes alwayes for all things vnto God

euen the father, in the name of Iesus Christ. To the Colossians he sayth: Let the worde of Christ dwell in you plenteously in all wisedome, teaching and admonishing your owne selues in Psalmes, hymnes, and spirituall songs, singing with a grace in your

hearts to the Lorde. To the Corinthians he sayth: When ye assemble togither, according as euery one of you hath a Psalme, or hath a doctrine, or hath a tongue, or hath reuelation, or hath interpretation: let all things be done vnto edifying. By which

wordes

wordes is declared, that singers of songs and Psalmes had their place in the Church.

But the west Churches more lately receyued the manner of singing. For Augustine testifieth that it happened in the time of Ambrose: For when that holy manne togither with the people, watched in the Church, least hee shoulde haue bene betrayed vnto the Irrians, he brought in singing, to auoyde tediousnesse, and to driue away the time. But as touching the measure and nature of the song, which ought to bee retayned in Musicke in the Church, these things must be specially noted, Saint Augustine in his booke of Confession, confesseth and is also sorie, that hee hadde sometime fallen, bicause he had giuen more attentiue hede vnto the measures and cordes of Musicke, than vnto the wordes which were vnder them spoken. Which thing hereby he proueth to be sinne, bicause Musicke and singing were brought in for the wordes sake, and not wordes for Musicke. And he so repented this his faulte, that hee exceedinglye allowed the manner of the Churche of Alexandria vsed vnder Ithanasius, who commaunded the Reader, that when hee sang, hee shoulde but little alter his boyce, so that he shoulde bee like rather vnto one that readeth, than vnto one that singeth. Howbeit on the contrarye, when hee considered, howe at the beginning of hys conuersion, he was inwardly moued with these songs, in suche forte, that for the zeale of pietie he burste forthe into teares, and for this cause he consented, that Musicke shoulde be retayned in the Church: but yet in suche manner, that he sayde hee was readie to chaunge his sentence, if a better reason coulde bee assigned. And he addeth: that those doe sinne deadlye (as they were wont to speake) whiche giue greater hede vnto Musicke, than vnto the wordes of God. Saint Hierome, and also Saint Gregorie say:

August.
li.9.confessᵃ

Aug.lib.10.
confes.ca.33.

Hieron.in
Epist.ad E.
phes.

Dist.92 tap.
Cantantes,
& in cap.
Sancta Ro-
mana.

Non vox sed votum, non cordula Musica, sed cor,
Non clamans, sed amans, cantat in aure Dei.

The

The voice though it crie neuer so cleare,
The Lorde delights not for to heare :
Nor string of Musicke very sweete,
Except the heart conioyne and meete.

Franciscus Petrarcha declareth that Athanasius did vtterlye forbid singing to be vsed in the Church at seruice time, bicause (sayth he) he woulde put away all lightnesse and vanitie, which by the reason of singing doth oft times arise in the myndes bothe of the singers and hearers. Gregorie also sayth : *Plerunque vt in sacro ministerio dum blanda vox quæritur, congrua vita negligatur,* Whyles the sweetenesse of the voyce is sought for in the holy ministerie, the life is neglected. Therefore sayeth Durandus : *Propter carnales, non propter spirituales cantandi vsus in Ecclesia institutus est. &c.* The vse of singing in the Church was ordeyned for carnall men, and not for spirituall mindod men.

Y O V T H. Let me heare then what is to be done and obserued, to the ende Musicke maye lawfully and fruitfully be vsed in the Church.

A G E. First we must take heede that in Musicke bee not put the whole summe and effect of godlynesse, and of the worshipping of God, which among the Papistes they doe almost euerywhere thinke that they haue fullye worshipped God, when they haue long and much sung and piped. Further we must take heede that in it be not put merite or remission of sinnes. Thirdly, that singing be not so much vsed and occupied in the Church, that there be no time in a maner left to preach the worde of God and holye doctrine. Whereby it commeth to passe, that the people depart out of the Church full of Musicke and harmonie, but yet hungerbaned and fasting, as touching heauenly foode and doctrine. Fourthly, that rich & large stipends be not so appointed for Musitians, that eyther very little, or in a maner nothing is prouided for the ministers which labour in the worde of God. Fiftly, neyther may that broken and quauering musicke be vsed, wherewith the standers by are so letted, that they cannot vnderstand the wordes, no,

though

though they woulde neuer so faine. Lastly, we must take heede, that in the Church nothing be song without choyce, but onelye those things which are contayned in the holye Scriptures, or which are by iust reason gathered out of them, and doe exactly agree with the worde of God.

Nowe to conclude this matter, I saye, that godly, and religious songs may be retayned in the Church. And yet I confesse that there is no precept giuen in the new testament of that thing. Wherefore if there be any Church, which vpon iust causes vseth it not, the same Church cannot iustlye be condemned, so that it defende not, that the thing it selfe of his owne nature, or by the commaundement of God is vnlawfull, and that it doe not for the same cause reproue other Churches, which vse singing and Musicke, or else exclude them from the fellowship of Christ. Yet this ought to be considered, that if we shall perceyue, that christian people doe runne vnto the Churche, as to a Stage playe, where they may be delighted with pyping and singing (and doe thereby absent themselues from hearing the worde of God preached) in this case we must rather abstaine from a thing not necessarie, than to suffer their pleasures to be cockered with the destruction of their soules.

YOVTH. What say you of Minstrels that go and range abroade, and thrust themselues into euery mannes presence and company to play some mirth vnto them.

AGE. These sort of people are not sufferable, bicause they are loyterers and ydle fellowes, & are therefore by the lawes and statutes of this Realme forbidden to raunge and roaue abroade, counting them in the number of Roges, and to saye truth, they are but defacers of Musicke.

Anno Elis-zabeth.14

YOVTH. Are there any other good exercises?

AGE. Yes, as Schollers to make Orations, to playe good and honest Comedies, to play at Tennis, and such like. &c. Notwithstanding in all these exercises that I haue spoken off before, this must I adde for your instruction, that none of them ought to be a hinderance or let to any man, from his duetie towardes

God

Gods worde.

YOVTH. Nowe that you haue declared to me what exercises are lawfull for the powers of the minde and bodie, I praye
you to shewe mee, what that playe is, which you call chaunce
or happe?

AGE. These Playes that depende vpon chaunce, are those
which we call Dice play, which kinde of Play is to be eschewed
and auoyded of all men. So Cato giueth counsell to all youth,
saying: *Trocho lude, aleas fuge,* Playe with the toppe, and flee
Diceplaying.

YOVTH. What meane you to speake againſt Diceplaying,
sithe so manye honourable, worshipfull, and honeſt men vse so
commonly to play at it?

AGE. The perſons make it not good, but rather it maketh
them the worſe: for it cauſeth manye of them (oftentimes) to
bring a Caſtell into a Capcaſe, a whole Manour and Lorde-
shippe into a Cottage, their Fee ſimple into Fee ſingle, with
other infinite lyke diſcommodities, according to the olde
verſe:

Diues eram dudum, me fecerunt tria nudum:
Alea, Vina, Venus, tribus hiiſum factus egenus.

    Sometime riche I was,
       and had thereof great ſpare,
    But three things hath me made,
       to go full poore and bare:
    Dyce, wyne, and Venerie,
       were to me great ſpeede,
    Theſe three did haſten all my woe,
       and brought me to great neede.

    Yet notwithſtanding, although theſe men that you ſpeake of,
vſe to play at Dice, and loue that game ſo well, yet in no wyſe
will be called Dice players, or Dicers, it is ſo odious a name, the
reaſon is, for that it is an odious and wicked play: ſo the thefe,
               the

the Queane, the Papiſtes, Murderer, &c. will not be called by that name, of that fault and filthie ſinne which they vſe, bicauſe they knowe it is moſt wicked and abhominable.

YOVTH. This fault of loſing their goodes, is not to be imputed to the play it ſelfe, but to them that play.

AGE. Yes ſir, it is in the Playe alſo : Take awaye the whore, there will be no whoredome : take awaye fire, there will be no burning : take awaye powder and ſhotte, none ſhall bee murthered : take away poyſon, none can be poyſoned, &c. take awaye Playe, there will bee no playing. This did Marcus Antonius the Emperour verye well ſee, who lying in his death bedde, ſayde to his ſonne Commodus theſe wordes : It is a moſt harde thing and a difficill matter for a man to kepe meaſure in libertie (of Playes) or to bee able to reſtrayne the brydle of things deſired, (vnleſſe the things themſelues be taken away that are deſired) for ſurely we be all made worſe, both olde and yong, by reaſon of this libertie to play at Dice, to enioye our owne filthie deſires.

Herodian. lib.1.

YOVTH. I praye you, who was the firſte deuiſour of Dyce playing ? It appeareth that it hath bene of a long continuance.

AGE. There are diuerſe opinions hereof. Some ſaye that it was one Attalus : Others ſuppoſe that it was deuiſed by one Brulla. Polydore Virgill ſayeth, that one Lydi deuiſed this among the Lydians a people of Aſia, of great loue and policie, what time a great famine was among them, that by paſſing away the time with this Play, they bare out their hunger the better, and their vittailes endured alſo the longer, &c. Others ſaye, that one Palamedes, being (in an armie of the Greekes agaynſt the Troianes) ydle, inuented this Diceplaye to paſſe the time away, and alſo to ſaue vittails, &c. But certainly thoſe that write of the inuentions of things, haue good cauſe to ſuppoſe Lucifer the Prince of Deuilles, to be the firſt inuenter thereof, and hell (no doubte) was the place where it was firſte founded.

Polyd. Virg. in lib.2. ca. 8. de inuentos toribus rer,

Ioh. Raniſius Textor,

For

For what better alective, coulde Satan deuise to allure and bring men pleasantly into damnable seruitude, than to purpose to them a forme of Play (which is his principall treasurie, wherin the more part of sinne and wickednesse is contayned, and all goodnesse, vertue, honestie, and godlynesse cleane confounded.

YOVTH. I assure you, I neuer hearde before, that Diceplaying was so w.cked, as you say.

Publius. *AGE.* Publius sayth: *Quanto Aleator in arte melior est, tanto nequior est,* Is much more cunning the Dicer is in that arte, so much the more wicked he is. There cannot be a more playne figure of Idlenesse, than Diceplaying is. For (besides that there is no maner of exercise of the bodie or minde therein) they vse great and terrible blasphemings and swearings, wicked brawlings, robbing, and stealing, craft, couetousnesse, and deceyte. Oh, why doe we call that a play, which is compact of couetousnesse, malice, craft, and deceyte?

YOVTH. What craft, deceite, and robbery can there bee in Dice playing? Are not the little Dice cast downe vpon the table, that euery man maye see them that hath but halfe an eye, and may easily tell euery pricke and poynt vpon them? And therefore I cannot see, howe any man shoulde thereby be deceyued, I suppose there is not a more plaine playe, and lesse deceyte (being alwayes before mens eyes) than is Diceplaying.

AGE. The blinde eateth many a flie, and seeth it not. For I perceyue that you are (or else you seeme so to be) ignorant of their skill and doings. If you did vnderstande throughly of their false Dice, cogging ternies, and orders, it will make you to abhorre, detest, and defie all Diceplaying.

YOVTH. Is there any more to bee considered in this Playe, than plainly and simply to play with two dice, and cast them out of our handes vpon the plaine boorde?

AGE. Yea, my sonne, much more, both for their craft in casting them, and making them, and also for the sundrie names of their Dice, to beguile the simple and ignorant withall.

YOVTH. I had neuer thought that there coulde be such deceyte

eyte in Dice playing, or that men had anye cunning or sleyght therein to beguile any.

AGE. For the obteyning of this skill (of filthie Dice playing) they haue made as it were an arte, and haue their peculiar termes for it. And a number of lewde persons haue and daily doe apply it as it were Grammer, or Logike, or any other good seruice or science, when as they associate togither with their harlots and fellowe theeues.

YOVTH. What haue Dicers to do with harlots and theeues?

AGE. As much as with their very frends: for they are all of one hall and corporation, and spring all out of one roote, and so tende they all to one ende, polely to liue by rauine and craft, deuouring the fruites (like Caterpillers) of other mennes labours: and trauailes craftily to get it into their owne handes as theeues.

YOVTH. I pray you shewe mee the occasion, why men so earnestly are giuen to Dice playing?

AGE. The first occasion to playe, is tediousnesse and loth-somnesse of good labours. Secondly, is couetousnesse and greedinesse for other mens mony, which couetousnesse, sayth S. Paul, is the roote of all mischiefe.

1.Tim.6.10
Ierem.6.13.

YOVTH. I perceyue by you, that there groweth greate and daungerous inconueniences and mischiefes by this Diceplaying.

AGE. You haue sayde truth. For it is a doore and a windowe into all theft, murther, whoredome, swearing, blaspheming, banketting, dauncing, rioting, drunkennesse, pryde, couetousnesse, craft, deceipt, lying, brawling, fighting, prodigalitie, nightwatchings, idlenesse, beggerie, pouertie, bankerupting, miserie, prisonment, hanging.&c. And what not? Saint Chrysostome sayth: that God neuer inuented Playes, but the Deuill: for the people sate downe to eate and drinke, and rose vp to play, in the honour of a most filthie ydoll, for when they had worshipped the calfe, and committed ydolatrie, they seemed to haue obteyned this rewarde of the Deuill, namely to play. Saint Ambrose saith also, that Playes and pastimes sweete and pleasant, when as yet they are contrarie to the rules of christianitie. Sir Thomas Eliot

Chrysost.in Mat.hom.6.

Ambr.lib.1. de offic.ca.23

Sir Thomas Elios knight in his booke of the gouernour.

D.   Knight

knight sayth to such as are Diceplayers : Euery thing (sayth he)
is to be esteemed after his value : but who hearing a man, whom
he knoweth not to be called a Dicer, doth not anon suppose him
to be of a light credit, dissolute, vaine, and remisse ? How manye
Gentlemen, howe many Merchants, &c. haue in this damnable
pastime (of Diceplaying) consumed their substaunce, as well
by their owne labours, as by their parentes, with great studie
and painfull trauell, in a long time acquired, and finished their
liues in debt and penurie ? Howe many godly and bolde yong
men (sayth he) hath it brought to theft, whereby they haue pre-
uented the course of nature, and died by the order of the lawes mi-
serably ? These are the fruites and reuenues of that wicked mer-
chandice (of Diceplaying.)

  YOVTH. Is it lawfull for any man to play at any game for
mony, to wynne it, keepe it, and purse it vp or no ? I pray you
let me knowe your iudgement herein.

  AGE. I saye generally, it is not lawfull to play for mony,
to winne it, and purse it vp, that is, eyther to lose his owne, or
winne others, to witholde it as good gaine.

  YOVTH. What reason is there hereof ?

  AGE. The reason is most cleare and plaine : First that play
(whatsoeuer it be) was not appoynted or permitted as a meane
and way to get or winne mony, but onely for exercise of the bodie, or recreation of the minde : so that whosoeuer vseth it to o-
ther ende, maketh it no game, but abuseth, chaungeth, and alte-
reth the nature of the recreation, into a filthie and vnsufferable
gayne, and therefore dishonest . Which (be they high, bee they

i.Tim.5.8. lowe) Christians ought to flee and shunne, as Saint Paule
August.in sayth, from filthie lucre. And in the Distinctions out of Augu-
Epist.54.ad stine, it is sayde : *Hoc autem iure possidetur quod iustè : Et hoc iu-*
Macedoni ii.
Distinc.35. *stè quod bene , omne igitur quod malè possidetur, alienum est. &c.*
Ca.Episcopus. That is rightly possessed, that is rightly gotten: and that is right-
ly gotten, that is well and truly gotten : therfore whatsoeuer is
possessed falsely and naughtily, is another mans and not thine. &c.
Tullie sayth also : *Nihil vtile est, quod non sit honestum,* Nothing

is profitable or gaine (to thee) which is not honestlye gotten: otherwise it is *Turpe lucrum*, filthie gaines. Furthermore, gaming was neuer allowed as a kinde of bargaining, traffike, or occupying among men: if wee eyther consider Gods lawe or mans. Amongst all ye lawes in the world, which haue throughly decided all meanes howe to get, and iustly to possesse other mens goodes, neuer make mention that gaming was a iust meane. The Romane law, which we call the Ciuile lawe, hath verye largely and diligently determined of it. But amongst all the honest meanes whereof the Ciuile lawe maketh mention, gaming is not mentioned, nor once within the compasse. Yet he speaketh of contractes in sale, of letting to hire, making restitution, and such like, whereby we may iustly haue and get that which is others: but there is no mention at all made of Play, or that wee may thereby wynne or possesse any thing. So that whosoeuer taketh and keepeth the mony of another which he hath wonne in play, withholdes it without lawfull cause, and therefore agaynst conscience, and to speak plainly, sheweth himselfe a flat theefe. If S. Paule forbiddeth vs to vse deceyte in bargaining and selling, what shoulde we doe in gaming? And if this shoulde be suffred, we shall bring in a greedie couetousnesse, in steade of the recreation of the minde, and to be short, a desire to beguile eche other, in steade of solace and pastime.

To gayne then by play, and especially at Dice, is as much as to steale and rob, notwithstanding any customes, euill vses, or corruptiōs of maners. One maister Francis Hotoman, a notable lawier and a christian, confirmeth my sentence and iudgement, & sheweth that by the meaning of the law, that gaine gotten & pursed vp by play, is forbidden, and to be condemned. And S. Augustine sayth, that ye mony shoulde be giuen to the poore that is gotten by play, to the ende that the loser shoulde not haue his losse againe, & also that the winner might be disappointed of the hope to haue that which he had so euilly gotten. Also it is very reasonable, that besides this losse, the magistrate shoulde put them both (that playe) to a good fine, to be bestowed to common vses.

Francis Hotoman in libi de vsuris, cap.2.

August.in Epist.54.ad Macedoniū.

For, I pray you what reason is there to turne that to couetousnesse, which was appointed for recreation and comfort of man?
The poore which are so many in the Church of God, and so ne-
dye, as all the worlde seeth so many small children that are or-
phans, lacking schooling for want of helpe, and that he whiche
counteth himselfe a christian and a brother to these poore, and ac-
knowledgeth them for the members of Iesus Christe, shoulde
play away and spende his mony at his pleasure, and shoulde not
Esay.58.7. rather giue it in almes to his brethren, which are, as Esay saith,
his owne fleshe? Alas howe dearely is that pleasure sometimes
bought of vs, and what shame shall we haue before Gods aun-
Mat.25.44. gels for such lauishnesse, yea before the poore people of God, as it
is written in Saint Mathewe. When riche Churles shall eate
Luc.12.19. and drinke, and after fall to play, like to that cursed man of whó
Luc.16.19. Saint Luke speaketh of, and in the meane season poore Lazarus
our brethren shall lye and starue at our doores, on whom the very brute beastes to their powers, bestowed their almes in licking
their sores, and we that are men of his owne likenesse, haue mony to play awaye, and can finde in our heartes to bestowe none
on them.

Luc.16.9.   Let vs according to the commandement of God, make frends
1.Tim.6.17 with our monye, not of such as wynne it of vs by play (for they
will neuer conne vs thanke for it) but of the poore people of God,
Prou.17.19. which cause it to be restored againe (at that great daye of Gods
iudgement) with profite and increase. Saint Augustine sayth :
August.de *Fœcundus est ager pauperum, cito reddit dominantibus fructum :*
verbis dom. *Dei est pro paruis magno pensare,* Profitable is the field of the poore,
sermo.25. and yeeldeth fruite very quickly to the owners, it is Gods propertie to restore great things for small things. Saint Augustine
therefore alloweth not that any christian man shoulde giue hys
mony to any Iugler, or Stage player, although they shewe vs
some pleasure with their paynes, much lesse doth he allowe vs to
giue our mony to a gamster that playeth with vs, to whome we
shewe as much pastime as he sheweth vs : Let me then conclude,
that which I haue sayde, is true : that is, that mony gotten and
                                                   purses

purfed vp by play, is flat theft : and to gaine by fuch meanes, is plainly to robbe, and to poffeffe other mens gœdes without iuft caufe, and againft confcience, bicaufe it is playne againft the commaundement of God, that fayth : Thou fhalte not fteale. *Exo.20.15.*
Notwithftanding, that there bee a confent of the Players, yet there is a burning luft and defire of eche others mony, and to obtaine this their greedie couetous purpofe, they vfe this wicked and craftie play at Dice to deceyue, which is called blinde fortune. For that purpofe Juftinianus the Emperour, made a decree that *Cod.lib.3. tit.vltimo.* none fhould play publikely, or priuately in their houfes. &c. Thus we fee what gaine and profit by play is gotten, euen as Chrift *Luc.6.25.* fayth : They that nowe laugh, fhall weepe, and they that nowe haue plentie fhall want. &c. Saint Auguftine to this fayth : *Qua eft ifta rogo animarum infania, amittere vitam, appettere mortem, acquirere aurum, & perdere cœlum,* What madneffe is this of *Auguft.de verbis dom. fermo.25.* men, to lofe life, and defire death, to feeke for golde, and lofe God.

YOVTH. They fay, they cannot delite in playe, except they play for mony.

AGE. I woulde gladlye knowe agayne to what vfe they woulde put that (mony gotten) vnto.

YOVTH. Peraduenture they will beftow it vpon fome feaft, or elfe vpon the pore people.

AGE. But I fay ftill, it is much better and fafer not to play for any mony at all, for that (as you haue hearde) it is not lawfull. Againe, it may be, that you your felfe are not touched with couetoufneffe : but poffible the other with whome you playe, is touched therewith : therefore let the occafions of euill bee taken *1.Thef.5.22* away, which otherwife are very many which moue vnto euill. And if there were nothing elfe to feare the away from this play, yet let them for Gods fake weygh this (as I haue fayde before) howe great the penurie and neede is, and what number of pouertie there is euerywhere replenifhed, that we maye fay as S. Jerome fayde : *Nudus atque efuriens ante fores noftras Chriftus in* *Hieron.ad Gaudentiũ* *paupere moritur,* Chrifte naked and hungrye, lying before our gates, dieth in the poze. The lawe of God requireth so manye duties, that not our whole life long is able to perfourme them: and yet will we bestow time in playing at Dice? We are other: wise sufficiently sicke with couetousnesse of mony, with ambiti: on to ouercome and excell others. &c. Why then do they stirre vp these diseases with playes?

YOVTH. They say, this is not stirred vp in them.

Rom.14 21
1.Cor.8 13.
Math.18.6.
Luc.17.1.
Marc 9.42.
A G E. Nowe they must remember, that they may be easily stirred vp, when they enter once in play. And they must see not onely to themselues, but that they bzing not other also vnto the same disease, foz though they know their owne minde & strength, yet they knowe not others.

YOV TH: What and if they will so playe their mony? are they not Lozdes of their owne things? They say, they doe no wzong to their neighbours, they take away no other man goods by violence, what then can be sayd vnto them?

Haggeus.
A G E. That is not true. Foz the Pzophet sayth in the per: son of God: The siluer is mine, and the golde is mine, sayth the Lozde. Foz you must note, that God deliuereth vnto vs his

Tobi. 4.8.
Eccl.29.12.
riches and treasure, accozding to his good pleasure, as vnto stew: ardes to vse them, and bestowe them as God in his wozde. com: maundeth. And therefoze they ought to vnderstande, that it is

Psa.4.17.18
Deut.26.2.
3.4.5.
Leuit.27.32
Gen.14.20.
Cap.28.22.
Exo.22 20.
Leu.27.30.
Num.18.22.
23.24.28.29
Mat.10.10.
Luc 10.7.
1.Tim.5.8.
Pro.3.15.21
Math.22.21.
Rom.13 7.
Deut.24.19
Leui.10.9.
Cap.23.2.
the dutie of the Magistrates, to see that euery man vse his owne things honestly and well. And they ought moze deepely to consi: der, that God gaue them riches and mony foz foure speciall cau: ses and purposes. First, wherewith they might maintaine pzea: ching of Gods wozde. Secondly, foz the nourishing and main: taining of themselues and their familie. Thirdly, to pay tributes, taxes, and customes to the Pzince, foz the better maintenaunce and defence of their people and countrie. Fourthly, to helpe the poze and needie members of Chzist. &c. those are the ends where: vnto riches is giuen vnto vs, and not foz to waste it foolishly at Diceplaying, and so put it to the slippernesse of foztune. Also it behoueth euery one (especially those that pzofesse the Gospell) to repzesent the image of God, who gouerneth and ruleth all things

with

with reason, mercy, loue, and wisedome. But so to consume their mony and goodes at Dyce, and vaine playes, is not to be as Lordes ouer their owne things, but tyrants and spoylers, and not to vse them with mercie, loue, and wisedome, but with vnmercifulnesse, hatred, and foolishnesse, to abuse them. And on the other part, what thing soeuer is gotten by this kinde of Diceplay, is *Turpe lucrum*, filthie gaine: and that gaine so gotten, shall be a witnesse against them at the last daye of iudgement, if they repent not, and it shall be gaine put in a bottomlesse purse, as the Prophet sayth, that is, they shall neuer haue ioy or good thereof, as the Poet sayth: *De bonis malè quæsitis, vix gaudebit hæres tertius*: Euill gotten goods shall neuer prosper. A penny naughtily gotten, sayth Chrysostome, is like a rotten apple layd among sounde apples, which will rot all the rest. Therfore we must hold fast and firmely determine, that such playes are very theft and robbery, and therefore ought not in any wise to be suffered, for that they are gouerned by chaunce and rashnesse, so that thereby goodes and mony are indaungered: and also for that it belongeth to the publike welth, to see that those things be rightly gouerned: For God giueth goodes to be spent to good vses, and not vppon vaine fonde abuses.

YOVTH. These Players are honest, substantiall, and credible men, and though they playe at Dice, yet they giue to the poore neuerthelesse, and paye their duetie to the Prince neuer the latter.

AGE. Their credites are much cracked that vse this play, so that they can not beautifie or garnishe it by no policye, but contrarywise, that doth altogither foyle them. And for their giuing to the poore, it doth no more excuse them, than if they robbed a man to giue to the poore. They saye, they giue neuerthelesse, I pray you doe they giue by that euer a whitte the more? If they doe, yet wee maye not doe euill, that good may come thereof, (sayth Saint Paule) whose damnation is iust. Yet I pray you let mee vnderstande what they giue weekely to the poore.

Marginal references: Psal.112.9. Tob.4 7.8. Eccl.1.1.2. 3 4 5. Luc 14.13. Cap 19 8. M: th.25 8. 1.Tim.9.18. — Habbac.2. 6.11.12. — Higgai.1.6 — Prou.21.17 Eccl.34.18. — Rom.3.8.

YOVTH. Euerye of them giueth accozding to his habilitie, some a peny, others two pence, another foure pence, and the best commonly giueth but sire pence.

AGE. What is this to the purpose, in respect of their playe, whereat they will not sticke to venter at Dice, v.s.r.s.rr.s. yea r.li. rr.li. at a cast, and will thereat consume rl.li. oz an C. li. yea all that they haue. rc. which is lamentable to heare and see. But whatsoeuer they giue to the pooze, it is done (contrary to the rule of Scriptures) grudgingly, murmuringly, and vnwilling-ly. Some of them haue lost as much in one houre, naye, in one quarter of an houre (at Dice) as they haue giuen to the pooze two. oz thzee yeares befoze. Is not this to be cozrected and amended (by the rulers ?) If they neglect it, no doubt God will be reuen-ged of it, it is so wicked and vngodlye. It is a woztde to heare and see what adoe the Magistrates haue to make them and such like to be contributozies to the reliefe of the pooze weekely, accoz-ding to the statutes rc. What ercuses, what allegations, what pzotestations, what loquations, what persuasions will they vse, who knoweth not? either y they are not able, oz that they are falle behind hand, oz y they are not somuch wozth now by a great sum as they haue bene, oz that they haue great losses, oz that they kepe some pooze man oz woman, oz else some fatherlesse childzen foz almes deede, oz else they giue euerye daye at their doozes to the pooze, oz that they will giue their almes themselues, oz that it is not giuen well. rc. Oz what not ? so they maye not giue to the pooze. But to giue and put into a boxe foz a Mumerie oz maske to play at Dice, they will not sticke at tenne pounde, twentie pounde, oz an hundzeth pounde, so franke and liberall they are to please their owne couetous desire, and vaine pleasure. But to helpe needy Chzist in his members, they are pooze and want mo-ny: but to the furnishing forward of Diceplaying, we haue mo-ny and golde plentie, yea, if nede be, their wiues also are allowed their rr.s.rl s. yea twentie nobles to maintaine them to play at Dice, supposing that it is a great token (to the woztde) of credite, & a signe of excellent loue betwene that is them, when in dede it is

btterly

Rom.12.8
2.Cor.9.7.
Prou.11.25.
Eccl.35.10.

btterly a discredite to both of them, and a token that they loue not in the Lorde. Thus we are wise(sayth the Prophet)to doe euill, but to doe well we haue no knowledge. Ierem.4.22.

YOVTH. They saye, it is written in Ecclesiastes, that wee ought not to be too righteous, nor too superstitious: for that were the way to bring in superstition againe, and to take away christian libertie. Eccle.7.17.

AGE. Saint Paule commaundeth the faithfull not onely to forbeare from that which is euill of it selfe, but euen from all shewe of euil. But these chaunce and Diceplayes that I haue spoken of, or any such like, are euill things of themselues, & not alone simple shewes (as you haue hearde before:) and in effect, I would faine knowe what ouerstrait rigour and seueritie of life we do enioyne to Christians, if we allowe them honestly and moderately to play and sport themselues at all other games, that eyther stand vppon sharpenesse of wit, or wholesome and moderate exercise of the bodie? Saint Chrysostome in his homilie of losenesse, in hys time, aunswering to like obiections, sayth: That when we doe restraine from the godly their superfluities, we meane not to bring them to too great straitnesse of life. To be short, christian libertie (euen in indifferent things) must bee subiect to the politike lawes of the countries, and to the edification of our neyghbours: therefore we ought much lesse to take libertie in such hurtfull things: Let reason (sayth Syrach) go before euery enterprise, and counsell before euery action. 1.Thes.5,22. Chrysost.in hom.1. Rom.14.16. 1.Cor.8.11. 1.Co.10.23. Eccl.37.16.

YOVTH. They say, there is no harm if they play at this game without swearing, chafing, or couetousnesse.

AGE. If there be mony layde downe, it is impossible that they shoulde play without couetousnesse and desire to win:which must needes be vnsemely (as I haue declared before) and vtterly vnlawfull. And where they say they see no harme: besides the great mischiefes (that is too great) in this Diceplay (as we haue sayde) this my aunswere is ready, that the ende of such games sheweth the mischiefe thereof. Therfore Salomon speaketh very aptly to this matter: There is a waye (sayth he) that seemeth right. Prou.14.12. 13.14.

right vnto men, but the ende thereof is the waye to death: yea, whyle they laugh, they shall haue heauie hearts, & the end of their ioy is sorowe: a backslyding heart shall be filled with his owne wayes, but the good man shall depart from him. And so it seemeth that they do but weene and thinke that there is no harme in it, being caried awaye with affections, but the triall proueth the harme too too great, and therfore good men can perceiue it.

YOVTH. They alledge that there is none but common gamehouses and tabling houses that are condemned, and not the playing sometimes in their owne priuate houses.

Cod. Lib. 3.
tit. vltimo.

AGE. That game (which is called *Alea*) is condemned, and not the house alone where the play is vsually kept, and what allureth vs to cuſtomable and ordinarie playe, but onely the beginning to handle Dyce in our owne houses? To say that there is a vertue called curteſſe, which in Greeke is called *Eutrapelia*, that cōſiſteth in mans ſporting and recreating themſelues togither: I likewiſe ſay ſo, but that vertue alloweth not to playe at ſuch deteſtable games, as this Diceplay is, but onely at honeſt and lawfull games, as are the Cheſſe, & Tenniſe. &c. or ſuch like, and alſo to doe that but at conuenient times, and that moderately, without any exceſſe. To be ſhorte, there is no vſurie in the worlde ſo heynous, as the gaine gotten by this playe at Dyce, where all is gotten with a trice ouer the thumbe, without anye trafficke or loane. Seeing therfore that theſe games are ſo contrarie to the worde of God, ſo hurtfull & wicked, and of ſo daungerous beginning and miſchieuous a conſequence, we ought vtterly to forbeare and deteſt them.

YOVTH. They obiect further and ſaye, that Diceplaying is not ſpeciallye forbidden in the Scriptures, and therfore they may vſe it.

AGE. So likewiſe there is nothing founde in the ſcriptures, ſpeciallly of Bakers, Brewers, Cookes, Sadlers, Shoomakers, Tanners, Clothiers, Taylers. &c. Therfore may they do in their occupations what craft and deceite they liſt, to deceyue the commons, as to vſe falſe and vnlawfull wares, to make vnholeſome

bread

bread, and drinke, and meate for the common people. &c. no wise
man will graunt them that libertie : and yet you shall not reade
of them in the scriptures, yet you must learne, that all things are
founde generally in the holy Scriptures, as in this : Whether ye
eate or drinke, or whatsoeuer yee doe, doe all to the glory of God :
Againe : Whatsoeuer ye shall doe in worde or in deede, doe all
in the name of the Lorde Iesus. &c. I praye you what glorie of
God is there in all their Diceplaying? nay rather, what disglorie
is there not? what swearing and blaspheming is vsed among
them? what couetousnesse and craft, what falshode and thecue-
rie, what fighting and brawling, what pryde and vplenesse, what
pouertie, shame, and miserie, with such other like fruites, I haue
sufficiently declared vnto you already, and therefore I am sure no
Christian man will say, that God is hereby honoured, but rather
dishonoured, and therfore to be left off, refused, and detested of all
good men. Yet by their leaue, this game of Diceplaying is spoken of in two speciall places in the Scripture, that expresly make
mention of it with as great detestation as is possible. The one is
in the olde Testament, in the Psalmes. And the other is in the
newe Testament in Saint Iohn, where he speaketh of the game
that was played for our Sauiour Christes garment, and plainly declareth that it was at lottes (that is at Dice) to shewe that
the Church of God shoulde first be bewitched with suche lyke
games; to make the breach first to all other losenesse of life, & that
the vnitie of the Church should be broken by such meanes. &c.

margin: Eccl.4.4 5.
1.Cor.10.33.
Colo.3.17.
Math.7.12.
Luc.6.51.
Tob.4.16.

margin: Psal.22.18.
Ioh.19.24.

YOVTH. Hath any honest man of credit and reputation bene
euill thought of, for playing at Dice, before this time?

AGE. That there hath, and not of the meanest sorte, but
Emperours, Princes, and Counsaylers.

YOVTH. I pray you recite one or two to me for example.

AGE. That I will. First the most noble Emperour Octa-
uius Augustus, for that he played at Dice (and that but seldome)
hath among writers in diuers of his actes susteyned (in hystories)
a note of a sharpe reproche and shame for his Diceplaying, notwithstanding that he had many great vertues. Cicero reproched

margin: Suetonius in
vita Augusti,
Imperat.
cap.73.

Marcus

Marcus Antonius in open senate, as with one of the notablest
faultes that he coulde cast in his teeth, that he played at Dyce,
(which he calleth *Aleam*.) Claudius Cesar Emperour of Rome
shewed himselfe to be a foole and a very blockhead (not onely for
his other vices) for that he played at Dice. Also the Lacedemo-
nians sent an Imbassadour to the citie of Corinth, to ioyne
friendshippe with them: but when the Imbassadour founde the
Princes and Counsailers playing at Dyce, departed without doing his message, saying that he woulde not maculate and defile
the honour of their people, with such a reproch, to be sayde, that
they had made aliance with Diceplayers.

K. Demetrius.   Also they sent vnto Demetrius the king of the Parthians, for
his lightnesse in playing at Dyce (in a taunt) a payre of golden
Dyce. For the better credite I will recite to you Chaucer which
sayth hereof in verses.

YOVTH. I pray you do so, for I am desirous to heare what
he sayth hereof.

Chaucer.   *A G E.* Stilbone that was holden a wise Imbassadour,
      Was sent to Corinth with full great honour,
      Fro Calidon, to make him aliaunce:
      And when he came, happened this chaunce,
      That all the greatest that were in that lande,
      Playing at Dyce he them fande:
      For which as loue as it might bee,
      He stale him home agayne to his countree.
      And sayde: there will I not lose my name,
      I will not take on me so great a shame,
      For to ally you to no hassardours.
      For by my truth I had leuer dye,
      Than I should you to hassardours allye:
      For ye that be so glorious of honours,
      Shall not allye you with hassardours:
      I by my will, or by my treatie,
      This wise Philosopher thus sayde he.

Cicero in Phillipica.2.

Suetonius.

Lacedemo-mans.

The

Looke thee howe King Demetrius
The King of Parthes, as the booke sayth vs:
Sent a paire of Dice of golde in scorne,
For he had vsed hassardie there beforne.
For which he helde his glorie and his renoume,
Of no value or reputation.
Lordes might finde other maner play,
Honest ynough to driue the day away.

YOVTH. This is very notable : but yet I pray you shew me what Chaucers owne opinion is touching Dice play?

AGE. His opinion is this, in verses also :

Dycing is very mother of leesings,
And of deceyte, and cursed forswearings,
Blasphemie of God, manslaughter, and waste also,
Of battayle, oughtinesse, and other mo,
It is reprofe and contrarie to honour,
For to beholde a common Dicesour.
And euer the higher he is of estate,
The more he is holden desolate,
If thou a Prince doest vse hassardie,
In all gouernance and policie.
He is as by common opinion,
Holden lesse in reputation.

Sir Thomas Eliot knight, sayth : That euery thing is to be esteemed after his value : but who hearing a man (sayeth he) whome he knoweth not, to be called a Dicer, doth not suppose him to bee of a lighte credite, dissolute, baune, and so misse. &c. *Sir Thomas Eliot knight in his booke of the gouernour.*

Nicholas Lyra (in a little booke of his intituled *Praeceptorium de Lyra*) alledgeth nine reasons against playing at Dyce. *Lyra in lib. praeceptoriū. in 8.praecept.*

YOVTH. I pray you let me heare what those reasons are?

AGE. First reason is : the couetous desire to gayne, which is the roote of all euill. Seconde reason is, the desire and will to *1.Tim.6.9*

people and take from our neyghbours by deceyte and guyle, that he hath. Thirde reason is, the excesse gayne therof, which passeth all kinde of vsurie which goeth by moneth and yeares, for gaine: but this Diceplay gayneth more in an houre, than vsurie doth in a yeare. The fourth reason is, the manifolde lyings, vaine, and vyle wordes and communications that alwayes happeneth in this Diceplay. The fift reason is, the horrible and blasphemous othes and swearings that are thundred out in those Playes against God and his maiestie . The sixt reason is, the manifolde corruptions and hurt of our neyghbours, which they vse to receyue and take by the euill custome and vsage of this Diceplay. The seauenth reason is, the offence that it giueth to the good and godly. The eyght reason is, the contempt and breach of all good lawes both of God and man, which vtterly forbiddeth this Diceplay. The ninth and last reason is, the losse of time, and doing of good, which in this time of Diceplay are both neglected. For these causes (sayth Lyra) Lawes were ordeyned to suppresse Diceplay. &c.

YOVTH. Surely these are verye good reasons to proue that Diceplay is a very euill exercise, and that in all ages and times it hath bene detested and abhorred.

AGE. You may looke more of Diceplay in *summa Angelica,* in the Chapter *Ludus.*

Dicing is altogither hazarding, the more studious that a man shall be therof, the wickedder and vnhappier he shall be, whilest that in desiring other mens goodes, he consumeth his owne, and hath no respect of his patrimonie. This arte is the mother of lies, of periuries, of theft, of debate, of iniuries, of manslaughter, the very inuention of the Diuels of hell. An arte altogither infamous, and forbidden by the lawes of all nations . At this daye, this is the most accustomed pastime that Kings and noble men vse. What doe I call it a pastime : naye rather their wisedome, which herein hath bene damnably instructed to deceyue.

YOVTH. I maruaile and wonder verye much that euer this wicked Diceplay could be suffred in any Common welth.

AGE.

A G E. It hath bene neuer suffered, nor tollerable at anye tyme in any good Common wealth. For the Greeke and Latine hystories (and also our owne lawes of this Realme of England) be full of notable lawes and examples (of good Princes) that vtterly exiled and banished Diceplaying oute of their seigniories and countries, and whosoeuer vsed Diceplaying, was taken, reputed, and holden as infamed persons.

YOVTH. I pray you declare to me some examples and lawes hereof.

A G E. Iustinian the Emperour made a decree, that none shoulde play at Tables and Dice publikely or priuately in their houses, &c. Alexander Seuerus the Emperour, did cleane banishe all Diceplayers, hauing alway in his mouth this saying : Our forefathers trusted in wisedome and prowesse, and not in fortune, and desired victorie for renoume and honour, and not for mony. And that game of Diceplaye is to be abhorred, whereby wit sleepeth, and violencsse with couetousnesse is onely learned. He made a lawe therefore against all Diceplayers, that if anye were founde playing at Dice, he shoulde be taken for franticke and madde, or as a foole naturall, which could not well gouerne himselfe, and all his goodes and landes shoulde be committed to sage and discrete personages, appoynted by the whole Senate, imploying vpon him so much as was necessarie for his sustinance, &c. Finally, next vnto theeues and extorcioners, he hated Diceplayers most, ordeyning that no Diceplayer shoulde be capable or worthie to be called eyther to any office or counsell.

Ludowicke king of Fraunce returning home from Damiata, commanded that *Omnes fœneratores, Iudæos, Aleatores. &c.* All vsurers, Iewes, Diceplayers, and such as are raylers and euill speakers against the word of God, shuld depart out of his realm. In the Digests, the Prætor sayeth : If a diceplayer bee iniured, he will giue no ayde vnto him, and if a man compell another to play at dice, let him be punished, and cast eyther in the quarries to digge stones, or else into the common prisons. Also in the same Digestes it is sayde : That if any manne

Cod. l. b 3. tit. vltimo.

Alexander Seuerus

Centuria. 15. ca. 7. fo. 749

In Dig. de aleatoribus, lib. 9. tit. 5, num. 1

strike

ſtryke him in whoſe houſe he playeth at Dice, oꝛ doe him anye wꝛong oꝛ iniurie : Oꝛ if during the time of their play, any thing be pilfered oꝛ ſtollen out of his houſe, hee ſhall haue no lawe at all foꝛ it at my handes (ſayth the Pꝛetoꝛ.) Alſo whoſoeuer lendeth mony in this play, oꝛ lay any wagers among themſelues, they are not firme and good, bicauſe it is a wicked exerciſe, not ſufferable, but puniſhable.

Conc. Liber. ſinū, cap. 79.

In this Councell it was decreed, that if anye Chꝛiſtian did vſe to play at Dice, & would not giue ouer and leaue it, he ſhould be debarred from the Communion a whole yeare at leaſt.

Decret. lib. 3 cap. Clerici.

In the Decrees, it is there foꝛbidden that Pꝛieſtes ſhoulde be pꝛeſent at Playes (*Qui Aleator eſt, repellitur à prmotione, nec debent inſpectores ludi huiuſmodi*) That Pꝛieſt which is a Dicer, let him be expelled frō his pꝛomotion, neyther ought they to looke

Diſtinct. 35. cap. Epiſcop.

vpon ſuch play. Alſo in the Diſtinctions, it is foꝛbidden thē to be dꝛunkards and Dicers. &c. And the Gloſe therevpon ſayth : *ſimiliter Laicus priuꞓtur aut verberetur,* Likewiſe let the Lay man bee

Cano. 41. 42.

reſtrayned, oꝛ elſe let him bee beaten and puniſhed. Alſo in the Canons, that are attributed vnto the Ipoſtles) this wicked Dice play is vtterly foꝛbidden. So wicked and deteſtable hath this play bene eſtemed ty all lawes. And at one woꝛd, this kinde of play (as it is repoꝛted of a truth) hath ouerthꝛowne the kings of Iſia and

Iuuenal. in Sat. 14.

all their eſtate : therefoꝛe Iuuenall counteth Diceplaye among thoſe vices that eaſilieſt coꝛrupt a whole houſhold, and is ẙ woꝛſt example that can be in a well gouerned houſe, ſaying :

If ancient folke befoꝛe their youth,
doe play at Cardes oꝛ Dice,
Their youth will frame to doe the like,
and imitate their vice.

YOVTH. I beſeech you let mee heare alſo what our owne lawes ſay againſt this Diceplaying.

An. 12. R. 2

AGE. In the time of King Richarde the ſeconde, all vnlawfull games were foꝛbidden vniuerſally, and namely Diceplaying.

In

In the time of king Henrie the fourth, Diceplayers fhoulde be *An.21.H.2.* punifhed by impꝛifonment foꝛ fixe dayes, and if the heade Offi-cers and Sherifes made not diligent fearch foꝛ gamefters, they fhould foꝛfeyte xl.s. And if it were a Conftable,foꝛ his negligence he fhould paye vj.s.viij.d.

In the time of king Edwarde the fourth, it was oꝛdeyned, *An.17.E.4.* that all fuch as kept any houfes foꝛ play at dice.&c. fhoulde haue thꝛee yeares impꝛifonment, and to foꝛfeyte twentie pounde. And the players to haue two yeares of impꝛifonment, and to foꝛfeyt ten pounde.

In the time of king Henrie the feauenth,it was alfo oꝛdeyned, *An.11.H.7.* that diceplayers.&c. fhoulde be fet openlye in the ftockes, by the fpace of one whole day. And the houfekeepers that fuffered them to playe, to paye vj.s.viij.d.and to be bounde to their good be-hauiour.

In the time of king Henrie the eyght, it was oꝛdeyned, that *An.33.H.8.* euerye houfekeeper that vfed to keepe diceplaying within their houfes, fhould foꝛfeite foꝛtie fhillings, and the players to foꝛfeyte vi.s.viii.d. and be bounde by recognifance neuer to playe any moꝛeat thefe vnlawfull games.

Alfo in the reigne of the fame king Henrie the eyght , it was *An.3.H.8.* oꝛdeyned, that if any perfons did difguife themfelues in apparel, and couer their faces with vifoꝛs,gathering a company togither, naming themfelues Mummers, which vfe to come to the dwel-ling places of men of honour, and other fubftantiall perfons, wherevpon Murders, Felonie, Rape, and other great hurts and inconueniences haue afoꝛetime growen,and hereafter bee like to come, by the colour thereof, if the fayde difoꝛder fhoulde conti-nue not refoꝛmed.&c. That then they fhoulde be arreafted by the Kings liege people as vagabondes, and bee committed to the Gaole without bayle oꝛ Mainpꝛife, foꝛ the fpace of thꝛee mo-nethes, and to fine at the Kings pleafure. And euery one that ke-peth any vifoꝛs in his houfe, to foꝛfeyte xx.s.

In the reigne of our gracious Queene Elizabeth (that nowe *An.E.14.* is, it was oꝛdeyned,that all thofe which vfe(to go to the countrie

and

and play) any vnlawfull games and playes, shall bee taken as
Roges, and to be committed to prison, and for the first offence to
haue a hole made through the gristle of their eare with a hote
yron of an ynche compasse. And for the seconde offence to be hanged as a fellon.

YOVTH. These are excellent good lawes, whereby I see that
in all times (this Diceplaying especially) hath bene abhorred, detested, and sharpe lawes made to correct and punish it.

AGE. They are good lawes in dede: but I feare me it may
be aunswered, as one aunswered the Athenians (who bragged
of their lawes) that they had good lawes in dede, but fewe or none
duely executed. For I see that a great many of our Rulers and
Magistrates, doe not onely neglect the execution of lawes herein, vpon Diceplayers, but are content to receyue into their houses very worthily, such loytering Diceplayers and Mummers:
yea, rather than they shall depart without play, they ioyne fellowship with them, and play at Dice themselues, whereby they
do great hurt to the people whom they rule ouer, as *Tully* sayth:

Tully.

Plus nocent exemplo, quàm peccato, They doe more hurt by their
example of lewde life, than by the sinne it selfe. Esaye the Pro-

Esay.1.23.

phet sayde of the rulers in his time, that the rulers were rebellious companions of theues. &c. Seneca sayth: *Grauissimus mor-*

Seneca.

bus est qui à capite diffunditur, It is a moste daungerous disease
that commeth from the heade.

YOVTH. It is most certaine that you say, and therefore the
more pitie: for in so doing they are nurses to foster their euill doings, and allure the people by their examples, as the olde saying
is: *Qualis præceptor, talis discipulus,* As the Maister is, suche
is his scholers. And therfore a greater account haue they to make
before the throne of God, at the day of iudgement.

Eccle.10.2.

AGE. It is very true, as Syrach sayth: As the Iudge of
the people is himselfe, so are his officers, and what maner of man

Syracides.

the ruler of the citie is, such are all they that dwell therein. Syra-
ches admonisheth rulers to be good examples in manners, lyfe,
and doings, that they maye shine, and bee as lightes before
the

the people, that they whome they rule, maye beholde their do-ings, and followe their good, iuste, and bertuous examples, saying:

scilicet in vulgus manant exempla regentum,
V_t, ducum lituos, sic mores cuftra fequuntur

Such as doe the people rule,
    accozding vnto lawe :
Examples they must giue to them,
    howe they shoulde liue in awe.
Foz as the Captaines trumpe doth sounde,
    so will his hoste pzepare :
To followe him where as he goeth,
    to sozrowe oz to care.

YOVTH. Is not this gaming condemned likewise by the ho-ly Scriptures?

AGE. Yes truly most manifestly.

YOVTH. I pzay you let me heare howe it is fozbidden by the holy Scriptures.

AGE. First it is ozdeyned against the expzesse and thirde commaundement of God, which sayth. : Thou shalt not take the name of the Lozde thy God in vaine. So that whosoeuer v-seth this chaunce of lottes in ydle and trifling things, taketh the name and pzouidence of God in vaine. Foz the lot is one of the principall witnesses of Gods power (as Salomon recozdeth) that it is ruled and gouerned immediately by his hande, power, and pzouidence. And therefoze we maye not vse lottes so triflingly, as it were to tempt God, and to trie what care hee hath of the wozlde, but onely in matters of great impoztaunce, and where his diuine will shoulde be extraozdinarilye knowne and vnder-stode, as in diuiding of goodes, choosing of Magistrates, and such lyke, to ende all quarrels oz cozruption of voyces, and not in sleyght things, as thoughe wee woulde make God seruaunt to our Pastymes and Spoztes, and trye what care hee hadde

Prou.16.53.
Cap.18.18.

Actes.1.26.

P.ij.   L.

of them. Secondly, this play is instituted contrarye to the true
nature and ende of that which we in Englishe call Play or Pastime, and the Latines call *Ludus*. And therefore the Playe at
Dice is a very corruption of Gods holy permission, & of true and
honest play. For all playes are appointed and lyked of men for
two causes onely : eyther for the exercise of the bodye (whereof
Diceplay is wholy contrarie, being a sport of a sorte of ydle vn-
thriftes :) or else Play should serue for the recreation of the
minde, and refreshing of our bodies, whervnto Diceplaye is
wholy repugnant and contrarie : for therein is no exercise of our
wittes, but we onely stay vpon the chaunce of the Dyce, whyle
as well he that winneth, as he that loseth, is amazed and vnsure of
his chaunce, but alwayes gapeth for the chaunce of his happe,
without any pleasure, but onely a couetous desire to gayne. Also
we see that the more they play at such games, the more they may,
without any such contentment or pleasure of the mynde as is
founde in other honest and lawfull games. Thirdly, the forbidding thereof by the Ciuill lawes, and commaundements of magistrates, maketh these Playes offensiue, wicked, and vnlawful,
though of their owne nature they were not so. For Saint Paule
1.Cor.8.13. sayth thus : Though I shoulde forbeare from eating of fleshe all
the dayes of my life, rather than offende my brother, I ought to
doe it : Much more ought we for feare of offence to forbeare this
play, in that it is nothing necessarie for the sustayning of mans
lyfe, nor of like commoditie to the vse of fleshe, which S. Paule
willeth vs yet to forbeare, if occasion serue. For there are other
Ephe.5.15. wayes to pastime and sport vs, than by those playes. Fourthly,
Colos.4.5. the spirit of God commaundeth vs by Saint Paule, to redeeme
2.Pet.4.2. the time that we haue lost in ydle and vnprofitable things, and
to bestow the time present in good and holy things to edification,
bicause the dayes are euill. For when God giueth vs leysure eyther to read his holy word, to visit the poore, to comfort the afflic-
Mat.25.36. ted, or to doe such lyke dutifull deedes, we ought to doe it quick-
Iames.1.27. ly, bicause that incontinently one let or other may happen, which
may withdrawe our mindes therefrom, a thousande afflictions
are

are present before vs, and it will be harde to recouer that whiche we so sleightly ouerslippe. But I pray you is that well spending the time and the leysure which God giueth vs to doe good in , to lose it in playing at Dyce, which I haue declared to be so offen- siue? Fiftly, the beggerly and greedie desire in that game doth so farre exceede all other, that there is nothing that doth more entise and encourage a man to play, than this Diceplay doth. And the reason thereof is manifest, that seeing the loser perceyueth that such losse happeneth not by the cunning of the Player, but rather by his happe and chaunce for that time, he hopeth to recouer hys mony by the sayde hap, which is likely to chaunge, being natu- rallye chaungeable, and therefore playeth on hoping for better chaunce, and so continueth, feeding himselfe with looking for the chaunge of the Dice: so as this game is proued to be the very oc- cupation of loyterers and vagabondes, but in playes of skill and cunning, the cause of the losse is soone espied and to be perceyued, and therefore hee that perceyueth himselfe to be the weaker, doth immediatly leaue playe. What shall I speake of the insatiable couetousnesse that is in this Play, while eyther partie seeketh to winne others mony, or rather the one of them to vndoe the other, and also go about to deceyne the other? What shall I speake a- gaine of the great and excessiue losses that haue alwayes bene, and daily are in the sayde play? Some play away their houses, horses, clothes : some all that euer they haue, or can borowe, ere they can leaue off, till all be gone: so entising and alluring is this game aboue all other, which causeth so many come to beg- gery, stealing, and finallye to that vntimely death of the gal- lowes. To this effecte, a certaine Poet and a Doctor of both Lawes, sayth :

Gal.6.10.

Sebastianus Brantan lib. Stultifera nauis.

> The damnable lust of Cardes and of Dice,
> And other games prohibite by lawe,
> To great offences some fooles doth attice.
> Yet can they not themselues therefro withdrawe,
> They count their labors and losse not worth a straw,

P.iij.   Caring

Caring naught else, therein is their delite,
Till Christ and health be scaped from them quite.

There is almost no maner of degree,
Man, childe, woman, poreman, or estate,
Olde or yong, that of this game are free,
Nor yet the Clergie, both pore Priest and Prelate,
They vse the same almost after one rate,
When by great losse they brought are in a rage,
Right fewe haue reason their madnesse to assuage.

And to be playne, great inconueniences,
Proceedeth to many by this vnlawfull game,
And by the same oft youth doth sue offences,
To his destruction, and all his frendes shame.
Often some by folly falleth to be a theefe,
And so ende in shame, sorowe, and mischiefe.

YOVTH. What say you to Carde playing, is that to be vsed
and allowed among men?

AGE. I tell you plainly, it is euen almost as badde as the
other, there is neuer a Barrell better Herring (as the Prouerbe is)
yet of the two euils it is somewhat the lesse, for that therein wit
is more vsed, and lesse trust in chance and fortune (as they terme
it) and yet I say, therein is no laudable studie or good exercise.
Diceplaying is the mother, and Carde playing is the daughter,
for they drawe both with one string, all the followers thereof vnto ydlenesse, loytering, blaspheming, miserie, infamie, shame, penurie, and confusion.

YOVTH. Is there as much craft and deceit at Cardplaying,
as there is in Diceplaying?

AGE. Almost one, I will not giue a strawe to choose: they
haue such sleightes in sorting and shuffling of the Cardes, playe
at what game ye will, all is lost aforehande, especially if two be
confederate to cousin the thirde.

YOVTH.

YOVTH. As howe I pray you?

AGE. Eyther by pricking of a Carde, or pinching of it, cutting at the nicke, eyther by a Bumbe carde finely vnder, ouer, or in the middes. &c. And what not to deceyue? And therefore to conclude, I saye with that good Father Saint Cyprian: The *Cyprian.* playe at Cardes is an inuention of the Deuill, which he founde out that he might the easilier bring in ydolatrie amongst men. For the Kings and Coate cardes that we vse nowe, were in olde time the images of Idols and false Gods: which since they that woulde seeme Christians, haue chaunged into Charlemaine, Launcelot, Hector, and such like names, bicause they would not seeme to imitate their idolatrie therein, and yet maintaine the playe it selfe, the verye inuention of Satan the Deuill, and woulde so disguise this mischiefe vnder the cloake of suche gaye names.

YOVTH. They vse to playe at Cardes commonly alwayes after Supper. &c.

AGE. I will condemne no man that doth so. But Plato *Plato.* sayth in his Banket, that Players and Minstrels that are vsed after suppers, is a simple passime, and fit for brutish and ignorant men, which knowe not howe to bestowe their time in better exercises, I may with better reason say the lyke by all Carders and Diceplayers.

YOVTH. What say you to the play at Tables?

AGE. Playing at Tables is farre more tollerable (although in all respectes not allowable) than Dyce and Cardes are, for that it leaneth partlye to chaunce, and partly to industrie of the mynde. For although they cast in deede by chaunce, yet the castes are gouerned by industrie and witte: In that respecte Plato affirmed, that the life of manne is lyke vnto the playe at *Plato.* Tables. For euen as (sayth he) in Table playe, so also in the lyfe of man, if any thing go not verye well, the same must bee by arte corrected and amended. &c. as when a caste is euill, it is holpen agayne by the wysedome and cunning of the Player.

YOVTH.

YOVTH. What ſay you to the play at Cheſſe, is that lawfull to be vſed?

AGE. Of all games (wherein is no bodilye exerciſe) it is moſt to be commended: for it is a wiſe play (and therefore was named the Philoſophers game) for in it there is no deceyte, or guyle, the witte thereby is made more ſharpe, and the remembraunce quickened. and therefore maye bee vſed moderately. Yet doe I reade ẏ that notable and conſtant martyr (John Hus) repented him for his playing at Cheſſe, ſaying: I haue delighted to play oftentimes at Cheſſe, and haue neglected my time, and thereby haue vnhappily prouoked both my ſelfe and other to anger many times by that playe: wherefore (ſayth he) beſides other my innumerable faultes, for this alſo I deſire you to inuocate the mercie of the Lorde, that he would pardon me. &c.

O mercifull Lorde, if this good and gracious Father, and faythfull martyr of Chriſt, did ſo earneſtly repent him for his playing at Cheſſe (which is a game without hurt) what cauſe then hath our Dice and Cardplayers, to repent and craue pardon at Gods hands for their wicked and deteſtable playing? And I pray vnto God for his Chriſtes ſake, that this good martyr maye be a patrone and an enſample for all them to followe.

YOVTH. Well, nowe I perceiue by you, that Table playing and Cheſſe playing, may be vſed of any man ſoberly and moderatly, & in my iudgement you haue ſaid well: for that many men who (by reaſon of ſickeneſſe and age) cannot exerciſe the powers of their bodies, are to be recreated with ſome pleaſure, as with Tables or Cheſſe playing.

AGE. The ſicke and aged haue more neede to pray than to play, conſidering they haſten to their graue, and therefore haue neede to ſay alwayes with Job: The graue is my houſe, darkeneſſe is my bed, rottenneſſe thou art my father, and wormes are my mother and ſiſter. &c. Salomon ſayth: Though a man lyue many yeares, and in them all he reioyce, yet he ſhall remember the dayes of death, all that commeth, is vanitie. &c. Yet I doe not vtterly deny, but that theſe kinde of playes ſerue ſuche, that

ſome-

Iohn Hus.

Actes and Monumẽts of the Church in the fiſt volum, fo.747

Iob.17.13, 14.

Eccl.11.8.

sometime they may be permitted, so that they bring no hurt, re-
fresshe the powers, be ioyned with honestie, without playing for
any mony at all. And that that time which shoulde be spent vpon
better things, be not bestowed vpon these playes in anye wise,
that henceforth (sayth Saint Peter) they shoulde liue as muche 1.Pet 4.2,3.
tyme as remayneth, not after the lusts of men, but after the will
of God.&c.

¶ A Treatise against
Dauncing.

NOwe that you haue so well contented my minde
as touching Diceplaying &c. I beseeche you let
me trouble you a little further, to knowe whether
Dauncing be tollerable and lawfull to be vsed a-
mong Christians or no?

AGE. If your demaunde be generall of all kynde of Dauncings, then I must make a distinction: If you speake speciallye
of our kynde and maner of Dauncing (in these our dayes) then
I say it is not lawfull nor tollerable, but wicked and filthie,
and in any wyse not to be suffered, or vsed of any christian.

YOVTH. Are there diuers kyndes of Dauncing?

AGE. Yea that there are.

YOVTH. I am desirous to knowe them, least I do (through
ignorance confounde one in another, and one for another.

AGE. There are Daunces called *Chorea*, which signifieth
ioye, bicause it is a certayne testification of ioye. And Seruius
(when he interpreteth this verse of Uergil, *Omnis quam chorus &
socij comitantur onantes*, that is: When all the Daunce & fellowes
folowed with myrth) sayth that *Chorus* is the singing and dauncing of such as be of like age. There is also another kynde of
dauncing, whereby men were exercised in warrelike assayres, for
they were commaunded to make gestures, and to leape, hauing

vpon them their armour : for that afterwarde they might be the
more prompt to fight, when neede (for the publike weale) should
require : this kynde of Dauncing was called *saltatio Pyrrhica*, because it was exercised in armour. Of those Daunces Plato speaketh largely. &c. There is another kynde of Dauncing which was
instituted onely for pleasure and wantonnesse sake : this kynde of
Daunces Demetrius Cynicus derided, calling it a thing vayne
and nothing worth . And if you speake onely of this kynde of
Daunce, I say as he sayth, it is baine, foolish, fleshly, filthie, and
diuelishe.

Plato lib.3.
de Legibus.

   YOVTH. Who was the first inuentour and deuisor of thys
latter kinde of Dauncing ?

   AGE. There are diuers opinions hereof. For as Solynus
sayth : it was first deuised in Crete by one Pyrrhus , that was
one of Sybilles priestes. Others saye that the Priestes of Mars
(called *salij*,) inuented it, for they were had among the Romanes
in great honour for their dauncing. Others doe referre it to Hiero
a tyrant of Sicilia : for that he to establishe his tyrannie, forbade
the people to speake one to another. Whereupon men in Sicilia
began to expresse their meanings and thoughts by becks and gestures of the body : which thing afterwarde turned into an vse
and custome. Some others suppose that men when they beheolde
the sundrie motions of the wandring starres, founde out dauncing. Others affirme that it came from the olde Ethnickes. &c.
But what so euer these saye , Saint Chrysostome an auncient
Father sayth, that it came firste from the Deuill . For when
he sawe (sayth he) that the people had committed Idolatrie to
the golden Calfe, he gaue them this libertie, that they shoulde
eate and drinke, and ryse vp to daunce . One Sebastian Brant
agreeth hereunto, saying :

Polyd.Virgil
.de inuent.
rerum. Lib. 2.
cap. 8.

Rodulphus
Gualterus in
Marc. hom.
51.c.p.6.
Chrysost.in
Mat. hom.6.

Sebast.Brant.
lib. Stultifera
nauis.

   The first beginning and cause originall,
   I saye the cause thereof is worthie blame,
   For when the Deuill to deceyue men mortall,
   And doe contempt to the high God eternall,

                         Vpon

Upon a stage had set a calfe of golde,
That euery man the same might clearely beholde,
So when the fende grounde of misgouernance,
Caused the people this figure to honour,
As for their God, and before the same to daunce,
When they were drunken, thus fell they in errour
Of Idolatrie, and forgat their creatour.
Before this Idoll daunceing both wyfe and man,
Despising God : thus dauncing first began.

Whereby you may easily perceiue from whence this dauncing came, euen from the deuill himselfe, for there can neuer come good effectes, when the causes are euill, as out of a stinking puddle can not come cleane water, nor of thornes men can gather grapes, or figs of thistles. &c. euen so out of our kynd of dauncing can come nothing but that which is euill and naught.

Math.7.16, 17.18.20. Luc.6.43. 44.45. Mat.12.33 &c. 34 Iam.3.11.12.

YOVTH. Why do you speake so much against dauncing ? sithe we haue so manye examples in the Scriptures of those that were godly and daunced : As Miriam Moses and Aarons sister tooke a timbrell in hir hande, and all the women came out after hir with Timbrels and daunces &c. Also Jephtah when he came at Mizpeh vnto his house, his daughter came out to meete hym with Timbrels and daunces. &c. Also the women came out of all cities of Israell, singing and dauncing to meete King Saule, with Timbrels, with Instruments of ioy, and with rebecks. &c. King Dauid also daunced before the Lorde, with all hys might, &c. Also all the women of Israell came togither to see Iudeth, and blessed hir, and made a daunce among them for hir. &c. And she went before the people in the Daunce, leading all the women, and all the men of Israell followed in their armour. &c. Salomon sayeth : There is a time to mourne, and a time to daunce. It is sayde in Saint Luke by Christe himselfe : Wee haue piped vnto you, and ye haue not daunced. &c. Manye suche lyke examples I coulde recite, to proue Dauncing to be laudable, and not so wicked as you seeme to make it.

Exod.15.20, Iudg.11.34. 1.Sam.18.6. 2.Sam.6.14 Iudeth.15.12 13. Eccl.5.4. Luc.7.32.

D.iij. AGE.

A G E. I perceyue you vse to reade the Scriptures, for you haue collected out many examples for your purpose, which giue you nothing at all, to maintaine your filthie Daunce. Herein you shewe your selfe lyke vnto the Papistes, for wheresoeuer they reade in Scripture Peters name, vp gooeth the Popes false supremacie. Wheresoeuer they reade this worde Crosse, they aduaunce out of hande their Rode and Roodeloft: where they read Light, they set vp their Tapers and Torches: and where they reade this worde Will, vppe gooeth their freewill workes: and where they reade of workes, there they maintaine merits: where they reade of fire, there they say is ment of Purgatorie. And when they reade this worde Vowe, they applye it vnto their single and vnchast lyfe. &c. So play you, and those that maintayne Dauncing: for wheresoeuer you reade this worde (Daunce) presently you apply it in such sort, as though were ment thereby your filthie Dauncings, which is not so, if it be diligently considered.

Saint Hierome sayth: *Nec putemus in verbis scripturarum esse Euangelium, sed in sensu: non in superficie, sed in medulla, non in sermonum filijs, sed in radice rationis,* Let vs not thinke that the Gospell (sayth he) consisteth in the wordes of the Scriptures, but in the meaning, not in the barke, but in the pith, not in the leaues of wordes, but in the rote of the meaning.

Y O V T H. I speake not of words onely, but I speake to proue Dauncing by certaine examples.

A G E. The Logitian sayth, that an argument made onely vpon examples, halteth alwayes vpon one foote, that is to saye, that it is but halfe an argument. As if he woulde say: We must not buylde and make a rule vpon examples onely, without there be some other reason and authoritie. And therefore it is sayde: *Legibus enim viuimus, non exemplis,* We liue by lawes, and not by examples. If then a Logitian so saye vpon prophane arguments, we ought a great deale more so to saye, touching diuine causes. And if a Logitian will not allowe an argument whiche is not made but vpon examples, thinkest thou that the holye Scripture doth admit and allowe it?

Y O V T H.

YOVTH. And why not, I pray you?

AGE. Bicause the people then woulde fall into sinne and great errours. As a man woulde saye: Abraham had the companie of his seruant Agar, and therefore I may haue the companie of my seruant. Likewise a man might say, that Iacob had two sisters to wife, and therefore I may also haue two. A man might likewise say: Abraham pleased God, in that he sacrificed his son Isaac, therefore I shall please him in sacrificing my sonne vnto him.&c. And so if we must argue by examples, without reason, and authoritie of holy Scripture, there shoulde be nothing but confusion in christian religion.

YOVTH. I pray you then, let mee heare your reasons to the contrary, that these examples and such like.&c. serue not for the maintenance of Dauncing.

AGE Neuerthelesse (that I haue spoken sufficient hereunto) yet I will make aunswere to your examples.

YOVTH. I shall giue attentiue eare thereunto.

AGE. First, that Daunce that Miriam Aarons sister (and the other women vsed) was no vayne and wanton Daunce, for carnall and filthie pleasures (as yours is) but it was that kynde of Daunce which is called (*Chorea*) for they did it in praysing God, signifying and declaring their great ioye, that Moses and Aaron, with all the children of Israell, were passed the redde sea in safetie, and their enimies (Pharao and his hoste) destroyed. &c. And the like order did Iephtah his daughter vse, for the victorye that God gaue vnto hir father against his enimies. &c. And so did the women in meeting king Saule And also Iudith, and the residue of the women. &c. praysed God for the victorie that Saule had ouer the Philistines. And Iudith with the residue, magnified God (as appeareth in the xvi. Chapter) for that the Citie of Bethulia was deliuered from the enimies, by the death of Holofernes, and so in going altogither hande in hande, reioyced and praised God in Psalmes. Also here is to be noted in these examples, that you alledge for Dauncing, that Miriam and the other women, and Iephtah his daughter, the women that daunced in meeting

ting Saule, and Judeth that daunced with the other women of Israell, for ioye of their deliuerye. &c. daunced not with yong men, but apart by themselues among women and maydens (which celebrated their victories) but seuerally by themselues among men. Also their daunces were spirituall, religious, and godly, not after our hoppings, and leapings, and interminglings men with women. &c. (dauncing euery one for his part) but soberly, grauely, and matronelyke, mouing scarce little or nothing in their gestures at all, eyther in countenance or bodie : they had no Minstrels or pypers to play vnto them : but they tooke their Timbrels into their owne handes (that coulde play) and not as our foolishe and fonde women vse to mixe themselues with men in their Daunce. And as for that place of Salomon that sayth : There is a time to daunce. &c. He meaneth this kynde of daunce which these good women vsed, which is a ioyfulnesse of heart, which bringeth spirituall profite, and not carnall pleasures (as our Daunces doe.) Also Salomon hereby teacheth vs howe we shoulde vse tymes in their order : Is when there is a tyme and cause to mourne and lament, then must we vse it . When God sendeth agayne, good things, we must also vse that, and to bee mery and reioyce in the Lorde. A time of sorowe the widow had in losing of hir groate. Another time also when it was founde, to be mery and ioyfull . Teaching vs hereby also, that sorowe shall not continue for euer, but God will sende, some ioye and comforte. So likewyse ioye shall not continue still, but God will sende some corrections to nurture vs. &c. Therefore you maye easily perceyue hereby , that Salomon meaneth by this worde Daunce, ioyfulnesse and comforte . And by the worde Mourning, hee meaneth sorowe and calamitie. &c . Also you muste note in these foresayde Daunces, that it was an ordinarie custome and manner among the Iewes , to vse suche kinde of godly Dauncings in certaine solemnities and triumphs, whē as God did giue them good and prosperous successes against their enimies. Are our Daunces applied, reserued, and kept to such

blest

Luc.15.9.

vses? nothing lesse.

As for Dauids dauncing before the Lorde, it was for no vayne pleasure and carnall pastime (as your Daunces are, or as Micholl his wife foolishly iudged) as appeareth by Dauids owne wordes, saying: It was before the Lorde, which chose mee rather than thy fathers. &c. And therefore (sayeth hee) I wyll playe before the Lorde. In that he daunced, it was done in two respectes: one for ioye that the arke of God was restored againe: the other for that God had exalted him to be a King and Ruler ouer Israell, and this kynde of Daunce that he daunced, may be called *saltatio pyrrhica*. Saint Ambrose speaking of Dauids dauncing, sayth: *Cantauit Dauid, & ante arcam Domini, non pro lasciuia, sed pro religione saltauit. Ergo non hystrionicis motibus sinuati corporis saltus, sed impigramentus & religiosa corporis agilitas designatur*, Dauid did sing and daunce before the arke of the Lorde, not for wantonnesse and pleasure, but for religion: not leaping and turning of his bodie with Player-lyke mouings and gestures, but did expresse his diligent mynde, and religious agilitie of his body. Agayne: *Est honesta saltatio, qua tripudiat animus, & bonis corpus operibus reuelatur, quando in salicibus organa nostra suspendimus*, There is an honest daunc-ing, when as the mynde daunceth, and the bodye sheweth hym selfe by good workes, when as we hang our instrumentes vppon the Willowe trees. In that he sayeth there is an honest daun-cing, argueth that there is a contrary dauncing which is vnho-nest: and no doubt he meaneth these and suche lyke foolysshe and filthie Daunces, as we vse in these dayes. Therefore he sayth: *Docuit nos Scriptura cantare grauiter, & saltare spiritualiter*, The holye Scripture teacheth vs to sing reuerentlye, and to daunce spiritually (sayeth he.) And that Dauids daunce was a spirituall and religious Daunce, appeareth by the Ephod that he put on. &c. If you & such like Daunccers (if you will nedes daunce) had that spirit that Dauid had when he daunced, in praysing and lauding God for his gret benefits, daūce a Gods name. M. Gual-ter sayeth: *Nimis friuolum est, cùm de choris sacris intelligi deb: a*

Amb. in Luci lib.6. cap.7.

Rodulphus Gualterus in Marc. ho.5 n cap.6.

in

in quibus vel sola mulieres, vel viri soli eximia Dei benificia carmi-
nibus ad eam rem compositis, non sine concinno & decoro corporis mo-
tu celebrabant, It is a great foolishnesse (to maintayne dauncings
by those examples of Marie Moses sister, Dauid, and others. &c.)
For their Daunces were holy and religious, in the which all the
women togither alone, or all the men alone (by themselues) didde
celebrate and set forth the goodnesse and benefits of God, in verses
made for those purposes, not without a comely and decent order
and gesture in mouing of their bodies.

Luc.7.32.   And as for that place of Luke, where Christe sayde : Wee
haue piped, and you haue not daunced. &c. serueth nothing at all
to maintayne your dauncing : It was not to that ende and purpose spoken by Christ, but Christ spake it against the obstinate
Phariseys, greatly accusing thereby the inuincible hardnesse of
their heart, he doth reproch them, bicause the Lorde had tried by
diuers meanes to bring them vnto him, and they with frowarde
and rebellious mindes and heartes refused and despised his grace
offered vnto them, as appeareth plainly by these words a little before : then all the people that hearde, and the Publicanes iustified
God. &c. But the Phariseys and the expounders of the Law despised the counsell of God against themselues. &c. Then Christe
sayde : Whereto shall I liken the menne of this generation. &c.
They are like to children sitting in the Market place, and crying
one to another, and saying : we haue pyped vnto you, and yee
haue not daunced : we haue mourned to you, and ye haue not
wept. &c. As though Christe woulde saye : Nothing can please
this frowarde generation. John preached the Lawe, and badde
them repent and mourne for their sinnes. I (being the Messias)
doe preach vnto them the gospell of ioye, peace, comfort, and forgiuenesse of sinnes freely, without their merites and desertes, so
that they will neyther mourne at Johns preaching, nor daunce
at my pype, notwithstanding I pipe ioyfull and mery things vnto them. Christ teacheth also hereby, that the songs of little children are sufficient to condemne the Phariseys and such lyke.
Christ therefore by this similitude sheweth what was the wonted
                                                                    pastime

wonted paſtime of children, and it ſeemeth to be taken out of the Prophet Zacharie. And as this was ſpoken of the Phariſeys, I feare me it may be likewiſe verified in vs, you may nowe eaſilye perceyue what Chriſt ment by this pyping and dauncing, not mayntaining thereby your fonde, fooliſhe, and vayne dauncing, but rather it teacheth you, that if you refuſe the ſweete pyping of the preaching of the Goſpell of Chriſt nowe offered (which wyll make your heart and ſoule to leape and daunce within you for ioye and gladneſſe) and followe theſe tranſitorie pypes to daunce after that tune and facion. You ſhall one day (if you repent not) weepe for your laughing, ſorrow for your ioying, hauing your ſwinging handes, and leaping legges bounde faſt and caſt into vtter darkeneſſe, where ſhall be weeping, wayling, and gnaſhing of teeth. So that in ſteade of great houſes and pallaces, you ſhall haue hell : for delicate fare and paſtimes, euerlaſting paynes : for pleaſant ſongs, wo and weeping.

Zach.1.8.5.

Mat.22.13.

YOVTH. You cannot deny but there was dauncing allowed of in the Scriptures, by your owne ſaying.

AGE. I muſt needes graunt, that there is dauncing expreſſed in the Scriptures, but I doubt whether it was allowed of or not.

YOVTH. You finde nothing to the contrarie.

AGE. Yes, I finde that dauncings were often times reproued : but neuer commaunded (in the Scriptures) to be vſed, as you may reade in Exodus, Eſay, Eccleſiaſticus, Romaines, Corinthians, Epheſians, Mathewe and Marke (which places, in the margent you ſhall finde them.)

Exod.32.6.
Eſa.5.11.12.
Eccl.9.4.
Ro.13.12.13.
Eph 5.4.
1.Cor.10.7.
Mat.14.6.7
Mar.6.22.

YOVTH. Although it were after another ſort and facion than our daunces are, yet you cannot deny but that they daunced. For it is one thing to reaſon and ſpeak of the abuſe, and another thing to ſpeake or reaſon of the thing it ſelfe.

AGE. I did diſtinguiſhe Daunces at the beginning of our talke. And I wiſhe in God, we might followe thoſe godly people, men and women, who nowe and then vſed dauncing : but yet ſuch as were moderate, chaſt, honeſt, and religious. So that

R. the

the men daunced by themselues, and the women apart by themselues, and did by such kinde of Daunces shewe forth the gladnesse of their mynde: they sang prayses vnto God, and gaue him
thanks for some notable benefit which they had receyued at hys
hands. But we reade not in all the holy Scriptures of mingled
Daunces of men and women togither. And therefore not onely
the abuse , but also the Dauncing it selfe ought to be taken a-
waye, and not to be vsed of any godly Christian, for that there
commeth of it all wantonnesse and wickednesse.

YOVTH. Will you say that Dauncing simply of it selfe is
vitious and euill ?

AGE. I say not so, if you speake generally , as you haue
hearde before : but if you speake specially of your kynd and fashi-
on of Dauncings (as it is nowe vsed in these dayes) I saye to
you, it is not to be vsed, nor the daunce to be allowed, for that it
is wicked and filthie.

YOVTH. What shoulde moue you to be so earnestly bent a-
gaynst this merye and pleasant pastyme of Dauncing, sithe so
many Noblemen, Gentlemen, Ladies, and others, vse it continuallye ?

AGE. Bicause that they that loue God with all their heart,
and with all their strength , ought not onely to obserue his commaundementes : but also to cut off all occasions, wherby the obseruing of them might be letted or hyndered.

Heb.12.1.
Math.5.29.

YOVTH. What occasion of hinderance or let is Dauncing
vnto the obseruation of Gods lawe and commaundements?

AGE. They are most manifest occasions of transgressions
of the lawes of God, they are snares and offences, not only vnto
the Dauncers, but also to the beholders : for they stirre vp and
inflame the hearts of men, which are otherwise euill inough, e-
uen from their beginning. And that thing which is to be suppres-
sed and kept vnder with great studie and industrie (as the lust of
the flesh, the lust of the eyes, and the pride of lyfe) the same is stirred vp by the wanton enticementes of Daunces . I maye saye
of Dauncing, as Saint Augustine sayeth of Drunkennesse,

1 Ioh.2.16.

O dolo-

O dolorosa saltatio, omnium malorum mater, omnis luxuriæ soror, August.ad fratr.in Ere⸗ mo.Serm.39.
omnis superbiæ pater, O deceytfull Daunce, it is the mother of
all euill, the sister of all carnall pleasures, the father of all pryde.
Undoubtedly, if a man will consider himselfe, eyther by expe-
rience, or by reason, he shall finde the lustes of the mynde not a
little kindled and inflamed. And he shall perceyue that men returne home from those Daunces lesse good than they were, and
the women also lesse chaste in their mindes (if not in bodies)
than they were before. Therefore perilles are rather to be auoy⸗
ded than nourished. Dauid therefore prayed vnto the Lord, and Psal.119.37
sayde : Turne awaye mine eyes from beholding vanitie. &c.
Syrach sayth : Go not about gasing in the streetes of the Ci⸗ Eccl.9.7.8.
tie, neyther wander thou in the secrete places thereof . Turne a-
way thine eye from a beautifull woman, and looke not vpon o-
thers beautie, for many haue perished by the beautie of women :
for thorowe it loue is kindled as a fire. It is sayde therefore, that
the sonnes of God sawe the daughters of men, that they were Gen.6.2.
fayre, and tooke them wiues of all that liked them . The eyes
are therefore called, *Fores & fæneſtra animæ*, the doores and windowes of the minde. Iob sayde (when as he felt the discommo- Iob.31.1.
ditie in beholding such vaine sightes) I made a couenant wyth
mine eyes : why then should I thinke on a mayde? As if he would
say : Sith I vse not these wanton lookes to behold vaine pastimes
& beautie, I haue no desire & lust kindled in me. So that you may
perceyue, nothing so soone quencheth lust and concupiscence, as
not to be present, or to behold such vanities. Otherwise as Salo⸗
mon sayth : He which loueth daunger, shall fall therein. Can a Prou.6.27. 28.
man (sayth he) take fire in his bosome , and his clothes not bee
burnt ? Or can a man go vppon coales , and his foote not bee
burnt ? for he that toucheth Pitche, shall be defiled with it , and Eccle.13.1.
he that is familiar with the prowde, shall be like vnto hym. Deute.7.8.
And for that cause Syrach sayth : Use not the companye of a
woman that is a Singer, and a Dauncer, neyther heare hir,
least thou bee taken by hir craftynesse. Sebastianus Brant
sayth :

What

What else is Dauncing but euen a nurcerie,
Or else a bayte to purchase and maintayne,
In yong hearts the vile sinne of ribandrie,
Them fettering therein, as in a deadly chayne:
And to say truth in wordes cleare and playne,
Venerous people haue all their whole pleasaunce,
Their vice to nourishe by this vnthriftie daunce.

And wanton people disposed vnto sinne,
To satisfie their madde concupiscence,
With hasty course vnto this daunce runne,
To seeke occasion of vile sinne and offence,
And to expresse my minde in short sentence,
This vicious game oft times doth attice,
By his lewde signes chast heartes vnto vice.

YOVTH. Whereas Dauncing is so agaynst maners, and do kindle lust, the same commeth rashly and by chaunce, but euerye thing is to bee iudged, not of these things, whiche happen by chaunce : but of these things which are in it of it selfe and by nature. For there are some so chast and vncorrupt, that they can beholde these Daunces, with a perfect and chaste mynde.

AGE. I graunt that which you say maye sometimes happen, but I adde therebnto also, that all accidentes are not of one and selfe same kynde. For there are some which happen very rarely. Other some which by their nature may as well be present vnto any thing, as absent. And some such as are wont to happen often times, and for the most part, these last accidentes ought in euery thing to be considered, and most diligently to be weyghed. Neyther must we take heede onely, what may be done : but also what is wont to be done.

YOVTH. I reade that Aristippus daunced in purple, and being reproued, he made an excuse, that he was made neuer a whit the worse by that dauncing : but might in that softnesse kepe still his Philosophicall minde chast.

                                                 AGE.

AGE. Demosthenes sayeth (and is also cited of the Lawyers) that we must not consider what some certayne man doth at a time, but what is wont to be done for the most part. Graūt that there be some one man or other so chaste, that he is nothing moued with such inticements : but howe are the people and multitude in the meane time prouided ? Shall we for the perfectnesse and integritie of one or two, suffer all the rest to be indaungered? *Vna hirundo non facit Ver,* One Swallowe proueth not that Summer is come.

YOVTH. If these reasons of yours holde true, then take away Sermons also, and Sacramentes, meate, and drinke. &c. For many heare the worde of God, sometime to their condemnation, and receyue the Sacramentes to their damnation, and many eate and drinke, and are drunke, and doe surfeyte. &c. and so dye.

AGE. You must vnderstande, that certayne things are profitable to the saluation of men, and are commaunded by the word of God, which things ought by no meanes to be taken awaye. And some things that of necessitie wee must haue, as meate, drinke. &c. to nourishe our weake bodies, or else we cannot lyue here. &c. And certayne other things are indifferent, which if wee see they tende to destruction, they are not to be suffred. We haue the lawe of God for hearing of Sermons, receyuing of Sacraments, to eate and drinke (soberly :) but for Dauncing there is no commaundement giuen by the worde of God. Wherefore these things are not to be compared togither.

YOVTH. It is well knowne that by Daunces and leapings very many honest mariages are brought to passe, and therefore it is good and tollerable.

AGE. It may be as you say (sometime) but we maye not doe euill, that good may come thereof. For you haue hearde mee say often, that it is euill and not good to daunce as you do. But I am not of that opinion to haue mariages contracted by these artes and actes, wherein a regarde is had onely to the agilitie and beautie of the bodie, and not vnto godlynesse and true religion. &c.

Demosthen.

2. Cor. 2. 15

1. Co. 11. 2).
Eccl. 31. 30.

Rom. 3 8.

Tob. 4. 12.
Gene. 6. 2.
Prou. 31. 30,

There

There are other meanes much moze honest, let vs vse them in Gods name, and leaue these as little chaste and lesse shamefastnesse. Let vs remember, that although honest matrimonies are sometime bzought to passe by Dauncing, yet muche moze often are Adulteries and Fozications wonte to followe of these Daunces.

YOVTH. You speake moze euill of Dauncing, than there commeth hurt by dauncing, as farre as I can iudge.

AGE. No my sonne, not halfe as much euill as it deserueth, can I speake of, noz yet can vtter one quarter of the wicked and filthie mischiefes that come thereof. Marke the effectes thereof, and then you shall tell me another tale. Is it not wzitten in S.

Math.14.6.
Marc.6.22.

Mathewe, that the daughter of Herodias daunced at a banket which the king made: and the king toke pleasure in hir (whome he woulde not openly without shame beholde, foz she was a manifest testimonie of his vnlawfull matrimonie and incest) of that Dauncing it came to passe, that John Baptists head was cut off at hir desire. &c. so instamed she the Kings heart by hir filthie and

Theoph. in
Mar.cap.6.

wanton daunce. Theophilact sayth hereupon: *Mira collusio: Saltat per puellam Diabolus: &c.* This is a wonderfull collusion: foz the Deuill daunced by the mayde. She daunced not rudely, as doe the common sozt of people, but finely, and with a comelye gesture with measure. &c. as some wzite. But that wozthie man

Erasmus in
Annot. in
Math.ca.14.

Erasmus sayth: *Non subsilijt, vt populus putat, quemadmodum gesticulantur in choreis,* She daunced not with silence and modestie, as the common people suppose, but she daunced as others vsed to daunce, with signes and outwarde gesture. &c. But howsoeuer she daunced, it was euill, as the effect and fruite thereof declareth. Thus you may perceyue what fruites you shall gather of this tree. Very well is it noted of Maister Rodolphus Gual-

Rodolphus
Gualter in
Marc. hom.
51.cap.6.

ter vpon this, what fruites come hereof: *Inflammatur enim libidinis igne concupiscentia, datur scortandi & mœchandi occasio, officij & conditionis suæ obliuiscuntur, qui mundo mori & Deo vni viuere debebant: accedunt sermones lasciui, promissiones inconsideratæ, amantium obtestationes, & periuria, & frequentes rixæ, &*

pugnæ

pugna incidunt, quas non raro cædes miserabiles comitari solent,

Concupiscence is inflamed (by Dauncing) with the fire of lust and sensualitie, it giueth occasion of whoredome and adulterie, it maketh men forget and neglect their duties and seruices, whiche ought to die fo the world, & liue to God: there are present wanton talkes and communications, vnaduised, and rashe promises, taking Gods name to witnesse in vaine, of the louers, wherby periurie is committed, and many times happeneth brawlings and fightings, by the which oftentimes miserable murthers are wont to be committed and done. Sebastian Brant also sayth:

Sebast.Brant. lib.Stultifer. nauis.

Such blinde follies and inconuenience,
Engender great hurt and incommoditie,
And soweth seede.whereof groweth great offence,
The grounde of vice, and of all enormitie,
In it is pride, foule lust and lecherie,
And while lewde leapes are vsed in the daunce,
Oft frowarde bargaines are made by countenance.

YOVTH. There doth happen no such thing as you speake of in our Daunces.&c. that lust is thereby inflamed in them that daunce.

AGE. If it be so, why then doe not men daunce with men apart from the women by themselues? And why do not the women and Maydes daunce by themselues? Why are men desirous more to daunce rather with this woman, than with that woman? And why are women so desirous rather to chuse this man, than that man to daunce withall, before all the residue; but onely to declare thereby howe they are inflamed eche to other in filthie concupiscence and lust. And I am assured that none of you (which are Dauncers) can denie this to be true, for that eche of you haue and doe daily feele in your selues this inflāmation whensoeuer you daunce togither man and woman.

YOVTH. Still I maruayle why you speake against Dauncing, as agaynste things whiche are of their owne nature euill

euill, and prohibited by the lawe of God. &c.

A G E. I saye to thee my sonne agayne, that things are not alwayes to be weyghed by their owne nature, but by the disposition and abuse of our fleshe. We cannot denye but that wyne of his owne nature is good, which yet, is not giuen to one that is in an ague, not that the wyne is euill, but bicause it agreeth not with a bodie that is in that maner affected. So the people of Israell made a calfe of their golden earings, to worship it, they sate downe to eate and drinke, and rose vp to play, that is, to daunce (as Lyra sayth : *Cantabant in choro*, They didde sing in the Daunce. And Thomas de Aquino sayth : *Surrexerunt ludere, id est, ludis facere sicut choreas*, They rose vp to playe, that is, (sayth he) they made playes after the maner of Daunces. &c.) So that you may see hereby that these Daunces are euill also of their owne nature, whereby good natures many times are corrupted by them, as appeareth by the effectes, both by John Baptist, and also by the children of Israell, and therefore I may saye of it as Augustine sayde of Drunkennesse , *saltatio est blandus dæmon, dulce venenum, suaue peccatum*, that is, Dauncing is a flattering Diuell, a sweete poyson, & a pleasant sinne, which will bring in the ende vtter destruction to them that vse it (if they repent not.) And where you say it is not against Gods commaundementes, that is false. Doth not the Lorde in his lawe commaunde, that ye shuld not couet the wife, maid, or seruant of your neighbors. &c. Much lesse then, that thou shouldest consent to thy concupiscence, that thou shouldest drawe and chose hir to thy selfe, to bee thy fellowe dauncer, which to doe, is not lawfull for thee. Also, when Christ sayde : He hath committed adulterie already in his heart, that looketh on a woman to lust after hir. What then shall we say of them, that not onely with wanton countenances, and filthie talke allure them, but also embrace them with their armes, handle them, and by all meanes prouoke thereby the burning lust of concupiscence, with their vayne kissings. Therefore Christe sayth : that tree which bringeth forth no good fruite shal be hewen downe, and cast into the fire. Syrach sayth : Sit not at all with **another**

Exod.32.6.
1.Cor.10.7.

Lyra in
1.Cor 10.

Thomas de
Aquino in
1.Cor.10.

August. ad
frat. in Ere-
mo. Serm. 33.

Exo 20.17.

Math.5.28.

Math.3.10.

Eccl.9.11.

another mans wife, neyther lie with hir vpon the bed, nor banket with hir, least thine heart incline vnto hir, and so through thy desire fall into destruction. What hurt then ensueth hereof, flat against the lawe of God, who seeth not?

YOVTH. You speake this as of your selfe alone. For I beleue none of the auncient fathers did euer speake against Dauncing, or that it hath bene forbidden by any Counsels, or mislyked by any good men, or by any good examples that you are able to shew and bring forth: therefore I wonder much of your straite order of talke agaynst our dauncing in these our dayes, I suppose it is bicause you are aged, and nowe are not able to doe as other yong men and women do, and this maketh you to enuy it so much.

AGE. Euery truth is to be beleeued: but euery beliefe doth not iustifie, neither shall your beliefe in this point. The cause why I speake against Dauncing, is verye euill gathered of you, my age is not the cause, nor my inhabilitie the reason thereof: but the cause that moueth me thus to speake agaynst dauncing, is the worde of God, whereon my conscience, talke, and iudgement is grounded, which worde is so pure and cleane, that it cannot abyde any impuritie or vnhonestie (which in your Dauncings want none, as I haue already declared vnto you.) And whereas you say, that I speake of my selfe alone without authoritie, is vntrue. For I haue already by the authoritie of holy Scriptures disproued it, (which authoritie of it selfe is sufficient, and to bee preferred before all authorities of men whatsoeuer they are. S. Hierome to this, sayth: *Quod de Scripturis non habet authoritatem, eadem facilitate contemnitur, qua probatur,* That which hath no authoritie out of the Scriptures, may be as easilye denyed as affirmed.) Yet notwithstanding I will proue by the auncient fathers, Councels, and many examples, that your Dauncings are euill, and therefore they inueyed and decreed against it. If I can declare this to you, then your beliefe (that you speake of) is vayne, and grounded vpon your owne ignorance, otherwise you woulde haue set your finger vpon your mouth.

YOVTH. I pray you let me heare it, & then I will beleeue it.

S.   AGE.

Hieron.in Math.cap.23

Iohn.6.29.
Luc.17.5.
Phil.1.29.

A G E. To beleue is the gift of God, and not of your owne power, therefore you haue not spoken well in so saying.

YOVTH. I pray you beare with me herein, for it was spoken (I confesse) very vnaduisedly, therefore I beseech you say on.

A G E. Saint Ambrose sayth (wryting to his sister Mar-cellina) myrth ought to bee in a cleare conscience, and a good mynde, and not in spiced bankets, and wedding feastes full of Minstrelsie. For therein shamefastnesse is yll defended, and vn-lawfull abusion suspected, where the last ende of pleasure is daun-cing, from which I desire all Virgins of God to keepe them-selues. For no man (as a certayne wise man of the Paganes sayth) daunceth, if he be sober, except he be madde. Nowe then, if that either drunkennesse or madnesse be reckened to be the cause of Dauncing among the Paganes, what then shall we counte to be commaunded in the holy Scripture: where we reade that Saint Iohn Baptist (the messenger of Christ) was put to death at the pleasure of a Dauncing wench? By the which thing we may take example, that this vnlawfull pastime of Dauncing hath bene cause of more hurte, than the phrensie of Robbers and Murtherers. This dedly feast was prepared with a kingly large-nesse and excesse, and watch layde when the company was at the most, and then the daughter which was hidde vp before in secret, was brought forth to daunce before the people. What coulde the daughter learne more of hir mother (which was an harlot) but to lose hir honestie? For nothing inclyneth folke more to bodilye lust, than by vncomely mouing and gesture, to shewe the ope-ration of these partes, which eyther nature hath bydde secretely, or good maner & nurture hath couered: or to playe castes wyth hir eye, or shake the neck, or swinge hir armes and heare. Wher-fore they muste needes fall into offense agaynst the maiestie of God. For what honestie can be kepte there where dauncing is? So then the King delighted with that pastime, bid hir aske what soeuer she woulde. &c. Thus farre Saint Ambrose.

Ambros.de Virg. lib. 3. ad Marcell. sororem suā.

Chrysost.in Matth.ca.14 S. Chrysostome sayth (speaking of the dauncing of Herodias daughter before Herod:) At this daye Christians doe deliuer to

destruction,

destruction, not halfe their kingdomes, or another mans heade: but euen their owne soules. For where as wanton dauncings are, there the deuill daunceth togither with them, in such Daunces his seruants delite. God gaue vs not feete to daunce with camels: but that we shoulde be companions with angels.

Ye haue hearde (sayth he) of mariages (intreating of the mariage of Iacob) but not of daunces, which are verye diuelishe.&c. For the Bridegrome and the Bryde are both corrupted by dauncing, and the whole familie defiled. *Chrysost. in Gen. hom. 56.*

Thou seest and readest of Mariages (sayth he) but thou seest and readest of no daunces in holy scripture. *Chrysost. hom. 48.*

Saint Augustine sayth: It is much better to dygge all the whole day, than to daunce (vpon the Sabboth daye.) Agayne he sayth: It is better that women shoulde picke wooll, or spynne vpon the Sabboth day, than they should daunce impudently and filthily all the day long vpon the dayes of the newe Moone. *Augustin. Psal. 32.* *August. de decim cordis cap 3.*

Erasmus sayth: And when they be wearye of drinking and banketting, then they fal to reuelling and dauncing. Then whose mynde is so well ordered, so sadde, stable, and constant, that these wanton dauncings, the swinging of the armes, the sweete founde of the Instrumentes, and feminine singing, woulde not corrupte, ouercome, and vtterlye mollifie? Yea, and further the Ballades that they sing, be such, that they woulde kindle vp the courage of the olde, and colde Laomedon and Nestor. And when the Minstrels doe make a signe to stinte, then if thou doe not kisse hir, that thou leading by the hande didst daunce withall, then thou shalt be taken for a rusticall, and as one without anye good maners and nurture. What filthy actes hereby (sayeth he) are committed: therfore as thou desirest thine owne wealth, looke that thou flee and eschewe this scabbed and scuruie companye (of Dauncers.) *Erasm Roter. in lib. de chs temptum &c. dial. cap. 7.*

Ludouicus Viues a learned man, sayth: Loue is bred by reason of company and communication with men (for among pleasures, feastings, laughing, dauncing, & voluptuousnesse) is the kingdom of Venus and Cupide. And with these things folkes myndes be *Erudit mulieris christianæ may. l. 1. ca. 14.*

entised

entiſed and ſnared, and eſpecially the women , on whome plea=
ſure hath ſozeſt dominion. O woman (ſayth he) howe miſerably
art thou entangled of that company, howe much better hadde it
bene foz thee to haue bidden at home, and rather to haue bzoken
a legge of thy bodye, than a legge of thy mynde? Agayne he
ſayth:

*Eodem libro
cap.13*

Some Maydes doe nothing moze gladly, and be taught alſo
with great diligence both of father and mother, that is, to daunce
cunningly. Feaſtings out of time, and pleaſant ſpoztes, and de=
licate paſtime bzingeth alwayes Dauncing in the laſt ende. So
that Dauncing muſt needes be the extreme of all vices. But wee
nowe in chziſtian countries haue ſchooles of Dauncing, howbeit
that is no wonder, ſeeing alſo we haue houſes of baudzie. So
much the Paganes were better and moze ſadde than we be, they
neuer knewe this newe faſhion of Dauncing of oures, and
vncleanlye handlings, gropings, and kiſſings, and a very kind=
ling of lechery: whereto ſerueth all that baſſing, as it were Pi=
geons the birds of Uenus?

What good doth all that Dauncing of yong women, holding
vpon mens armes, that they may hop the higher? What mea=
neth that ſhaking vnto midnight, and neuer weary, which if they
were deſired to go but to the next Churche, they were not able,
except they were caried on hozſebacke, oz in a chariot: who would
not thinke them out of their wittes?

I remember (ſayth he(that I heard one vpon a time ſay, that
there were certaine men bzought out of a farre countrie into our
partes of the wozlde, whiche when they ſawe women daunce,
they ranne awaye wonderouſlye afrayde, crying out that they
thought the women were taken with an vncoth kynde of phzen=
ſie. And to ſaye good ſooth, who woulde not recken women fran=
tike when they daunce, if hee had neuer ſeene woman daunce
befoze?

And it is a wozld to ſee, howe demurely and ſadly ſome ſit be=
holding them that daunce, and with what geſture, pace, and mo=
uing of the bodie, & with what ſober footing ſome of them daunce.
                                                                        Where=

Wherein also a man may espie a great part of their follie, that go about to handle such a foolishe and madde thing so sadly: neyther see themselues haue a matter in hande without anye wisedome, nor any thing worth, but as Cicero sayth, a companion of vices. What holy woman did wee euer reade of, that was a Dauncer? Or what woman nowe a dayes (that is sadde and wyse) will be knowne to haue skill of Dauncing? &c. For what chastitie of body and minde can be there, where they shall see so many mens bodies, and haue their myndes entised by the windowes of their eyes, and by the meanes of the most subtill artificer the Deuill. Thus farre Ludouicus Viues.

Maister Marlorat (a famous man) sayth : Whatsoeuer they are, that haue had any care of grauitie and honestie, haue vtterly condemned this filthie dauncing, and especially in Maidens. *Marlorat in Math.cap.14*

Maister Bullinger sayth : There followeth (in Feastings) vnshamefast Dauncing, which is the roote of all filthinesse and wantonnesse. *Bullinger in Mat.c.19.14.*

Maister Rodulphus Gualter, an excellent learned man sayth: Dauncings (sayth he) which we nowe a dayes vse, came from the Gentiles and Heathens first vnto vs. When as they vsed alwayes at celebrating of their sacrifices to doe it with Dauncings vnto their false Gods. Which the Israelites seemed to imitate when as they daunced about the golden calfe. &c. Afterwards this dauncing began to be vsed publikely in Playes, before the face of the people, of whome afterwarde the women learned it, and exercised it, least they shoulde be accounted no bodie. Then when shame and honestie began to decay, women also and Maydens vsed to daunce, and had their proper daunces appointed them. At last (when all shame in deede was past) by reason of the long vse and time of their dauncing, this encreased and went forwarde, that men and women being mixt, daunced togither. Of which there can bee no more vncomelynesse shewed, than to see men and women daunce togither, hande in hande, to leade and carie them about, that the beholders of them may see the quickenesse and agilitie of their bodies, by wanton mouings and ge- *Rodolphus Gualterus in Mire.cap.6. hom.51.*

S.iij.   stures.

1.Thes.5.22

Ephe.5.3.4

stures. Contrarie to that Saint Paule sayth : Abstaine from all appearance of euill. &c. and that no filthynesse, neyther foolishe talking, neyther ieasting, which are things not comely, neyther fornication and all vncleannesse, or couetousnesse, be once named among you, as becommeth Saintes.&c. By these Dauncings, concupiscence is inflamed with the fire of carnall lust, thereof commeth also whoredomes, and adulterie, neglecting of our duties and seruices to God and man. By Dauncing commeth filthie talke and communication, vnaduised promises, craftie bargaynes and contractes, periuries, brawlings, and fightings, and many times mischieuous murthers are wont to be done in dauncings.&c.

M.Caluin. in
Psal.30.

Maister Caluin vpon these words of Dauid : Thou hast turned my mourning into dauncing.&c. sayth:By the word (dauncing) there is not ment euery maner of wanton or ruffianly leaping & friskking, but a sober and holy vtterance of gladnesse, suche as the holy Scripture maketh mention of, when Dauid conueyed the arke of couenant into his place.

M.Caluin.in
8.b cap.22.
Serm.78.

He writing vpon these words (They send forth their little ones like shepe)& their children daunce.They play vpon the Taber and the Harpe.&c.) sayth: We see it is no noueltie in the children of this worlde, to exceede measure in the vanities which God condemneth, as in dauncing, and suche other like loosenesse . It hath bene so at all times. For the deuill (all whose driftes tende to blinde men, and to drawe them from the regarding of God, and from the spirituall lyfe) hath had these knacks from time to time, and men haue willingly followed that which they haue lyked of, and which pleased the flesh.Therefore whereas nowe a dayes we see many seeke nothing but to royst it, insomuche as they haue none other countenance, but in seeking to hoppe and daunce like stray beastes, and to doe suche other like things. Let vs vnderstande that it is not of late beginning, but that the deuill hath raygned at all times. Howbeit, let vs knowe also, that the euill is neuer the more to be excused for the auncientnesse of it . Men haue alwayes done so : yea, and that was bicause the deuill hath alwayes

alwayes reigned : but muſt God therfore be quite diſpoſſeſſed?

Muſicke of it ſelfe cannot be condemned: but foraſmuch as the worlde doth almoſt alway abuſe it, we ought to be ſo much the more circumſpect, we ſee at this daye that they which vſe Muſicke doe ſwell with poyſon againſt God, they become hard hearted, they will haue their ſongs, yea, and what maner of ſongs? Full of all villanie and ribauldrie. And afterwarde they fall to Dauncing, which is the chiefeſt miſchiefe of all. For there is alwayes ſuch vnchaſt behauiour in dauncing, that of it ſelfe, and as they abuſe it (to ſpeake the truth at one worde) it is nothing but an enticement to whoredome. *Calvin Iohn in his do. Ser. vpon the 23. Cap.*

Wherefore we ought to take warning to reſtrayne our ſelues, and whereas we ſee there are manye whoſe whole delight is to ſeeke ſuch paſtymes, let vs ſaye, a miſchiefe on them. And if we will not haue the ſame curſe to light vppon our ſelues : lette vs learne to abſent our ſelues from ſuch looſe and wanton paſtimes: but let vs rather aduiſedly reſtrayne our ſelues, and ſet God alwayes before our eyes, to the ende that hee maye bleſſe oure myrth, and we ſo vſe his benefites, as wee maye neuer ceaſe to trauaile vp to heauenwarde, ſo muſt we apply all our myrth to this ende, namelye that there maye bee a melodye ſounding in vs, whereby the name of God maye be bleſſed and glorified in our Lorde Ieſus Chriſt. *In his 73. Serm. vppon the 21. cap.*

To Muſicke belongeth the arte of Dauncing, very acceptable to Maydens and Louers, which they learne with great care, and withoute tediouſneſſe doe prolong it vntill midnight, and with great diligence doe deuiſe to daunce wyth framed geſtures, and with meaſurable paces to the ſounde of the Cymball, Harpe, or Flute, and doe as they thinke, very wiſely, and ſubtilly, the fondeſt thing of all other, and little differing from madneſſe, whiche except it were tempered with the ſounde of Inſtrumentes, and as it is ſayde, if vanitie did not commende vanitie, there ſhould be no ſight more ridiculous, nor more out of order than Dauncing : this is a libertie to wantonneſſe, a friende to wickedneſſe, a prouocation to fleſhlye luſt, enimie to chaſtitie, and a paſtime *Henricus Cornelius Agrippa.*

vnworthy

vnworthye of all honest persons. There oftentimes a matrone (as Petrarcha sayth) hath lost hir long preserued honor: oftentimes the vnhapple mayden hath there learned that whereof she had bene better to be ignorant: there the fame and honestie of many women is lost. Infinite frō thence haue returned home vnchast, many with a doubtfull minde, but none chaste in thought and dede. And we haue often seene that womanlike honestie in Dauncing hath bene throwne downe to the grounde, and always vehemently prouoked and assaulted: yet some of the Greeke writers haue commended it, as they haue many filthie and wicked things. But it is no maruaile that the Greekes doe in this sorte studie Philosophie, which haue made the Goddes authors of Adulterie, of whoredome, of murther, and finallye of all wickednesse. They haue written many bookes of Dauncing, in whiche is contayned all the kindes, qualities, and measures, and haue reckened vp the names of them, and of what sorte euerye one of them shoulde be, and who inuented it: wherefore I will speake no further of them. The auncient Romaines, graue men by reason of their wisedome and authoritie did refuse all Dauncing, and no honest matrone was commended among them for dauncing.

Dauncing is the vilest bice of all, and truly it cannot easily be sayde what mischiefes the sight, and the hearing do receyue hereby, which afterwarde be the causes of communication and embracing. They daunce with disordinate gestures, and with monstrous thumping of the feete, to pleasaunt soundes, to wanton songs, to dishonest verses. Maydens and matrones are groped and handled with vnchast handes, and kissed, and dishonestly embraced: and the things which nature hath hidden, modestie couered, are then oftentimes by meanes of lasciuiousnesse made naked, and ribauldrie vnder the colour of Pastime is dissembled. In exercise doubtlesse not descended from heauen, but by the Deuilles of hell deuised, to the iniurie of the Diuinitie, when the people of Israell erected a calfe in the desert, whiche after they had done sacrifice, began to eate and drinke, and afterwarde rose vp to sport them-

themselues, and singing, daunced in a rounde.

I coulde alledge you many moe, if I thought these did not satisfie your minde.

YOVTH. Satisfie, quoth you, yea, I assure you, they haue euen cloyed me and filled me to the full, I neuer hearde so many woorthy fathers alledged, as you haue done, both of olde and later writers, against Dauncing, which begynneth to make mee lothe and euen detest this vice and filthie Dauncing : Yet for promise sake, I pray you let me heare what Councels and examples there are against this dauncing.

AGE. In the Councell of Laoditia (holden in the yeare of our Lorde God 364. vnder Pope Liberius) it was decreed thus : *Conc. Laodis cense. ca. 53.* It is not meete for Christian men to daunce at their mariages. Let them dyne and suppe grauely and moderately, giuing thāks vnto God for the benefite of mariages. Let the Cleargie aryse and go their wayes, when the players on the Instruments (whiche serue for Dauncing) doe begynne to playe, least by their presence they shoulde seeme to allowe that wantonnesse.

In this Councell (which was holden in the time of *Theodoricus* the king) it was decreed, namely that no Christian shoulo daunce at any mariages, or at any other time. *Concilium Illerdense.*

Iustinian the Emperour made a decree, saying : We wyll not haue men giue themselues vnto voluptuousnesse, wherefore it shall not be lawfull in the feast dayes to vse any dauncings, whether they be for lustes sake, or whether they be done for pleasures sake. *Iustinian in code, titu. de f. riis, in lege die. fest.*

Emilius Probus (in the lyfe of *Epiminonda*) sayth : That to sing & to daunce was not very honorable among the Romaines, when the Grecians had in it great estimation. *Emil. Probus*

Salust writeth, that Sempronia (a certayne lasciuious and vnchast woman) was taught to sing and daunce more elegantlye than became an honest matrone : saying also, that singing and dauncing are the instruments of lecherie. *Salust.*

Cicero sayth, that an honest and good man will not daunce, *Cicer. lib. 3. de officiis.*

in the market place, although he might by that meanes come to great possessions. And in his oration (that he made after his returne into the Senate) he calleth Tulus Gabinius in reproche, *Saltator Calamistratus*, a fine mincing Dauncer. It was also obiected to Lucius Murena for a great fault, because he had daunced in Asia. The same thing also was obiected vnto the king Deiotarus. Also Cicero aunswering for Murea, sayd: No man dauncceth being sober, vnlesse peradventure he be madde, neyther being alone, neyther in the fieldes, neyther yet at a moderate and honest banket. He did vpbraide and cast Anthonie in the teeth for his wicked dauncing. The Poet Brant sayth:

Seb:st.Brant
in Stuli.fera
B.16 b.

> Than dauncing, in earth no game more damnable,
> It seemeth no peace, but battaile openly.
> They that it vse, of mynde seeme vnstable,
> As madde folke running with clamour, shout and crie:
> What place is voyde of this furious folly?
> None, so that I doubt within a whyle,
> These follies the holy Churche shall defile.

YOVTH. You haue alledged strong authorities agaynst this dauncing, whereby I doe taste howe bitter it is vnto me, for I perceyue by you howe full of filthinesse and wickednesse it is.

2.Cor.6.17.
Esai.52.11.

AGE. It is most certayne, that it is full of all wickednesse: therefore come you away from it, and vse it no more, nor haue you any pleasure in suche workes of filthynesse, as the olde saying is:

> He that will none euill do,
> Must doe nothing belonging therto.

August.in
Epist.144.

Saint Augustine sayth: *Nam qui gehennas metuit, non peccare metuit sed ardere: ille autem peccare metuit, qui peccatum ipsum sicut gehennas odit. Tantum porro quisque peccatum odit, quantum iustitiam diligit,* He that feareth hell, feareth not to sinne, but to burne: Therefore he feareth to sinne, that hateth the very sinne

it

it selfe as he hateth hell. So much doth euery man therefore hate sinne, as he loueth righteousnesse. So Horace sayth: The wicked feareth to sinne, bicause of punishment : the godly man hateth to sinne, for the loue of vertue, according to this saying :

> If I knewe that God woulde forgiue sinne,
> and that men shoulde not knowe it :
> Yet for the vilenesse of sinne
> I woulde not commit it.

YOVTH. These your sayings haue pierced my hearte, and done me very much good, I pray God that I maye followe this good counsell of yours, for I see nowe, that we must and ought to walke in a vertuous life and conuersation, that are baptised into Iesus Christ. *Rom.6.4.*

AGE. You haue sayde right : and therfore you must vnderstande that there bee three kindes of liues : One is occupied in action and doing : the seconde in knowledge and studie : the third in oblectation and fruition of pleasures and wanton pastimes. Of which, the last kinde of lyfe, delicious, voluptuous, or giuen to pleasures, is beastlike, brutishe, abiect, vile, vnworthy the excellencie of man. Therefore Paule sayth (vnto all suche as are come to the knowledge of Christ) The night is past, and the day is at hande : Let vs therefore cast away the workes of darkenesse, and let vs put on the armour of light. So that we walke honestly as in the dayes tyme, not in ryot and drunkennesse, neyther in chambering and wantonnesse, nor in striuing and enuying. &c. Neyther in filthinesse, neyther foolishe talking, neyther ieasting, which are not comely, but rather giuing of thankes. It is sufficient (sayth Saint Peter) that wee haue spent the tyme past of our lyfe, after the lustes of the Gentyles, walking in wantonnesse, lustes, drunkennesse, in gluttonie, drinkings, and in abhominable ydolatries. Therefore (sayth he) let vs henceforwarde liue (as much time as remayneth in the flesh) not after the lusts of men, but after the will of God. And whatsoeuer we doe, let vs doe all to the glorie of God. *Rom..3.12. 13 Ephes.5.4. 1.Pet 4.3. Ephes.4.23. 1.Cor.10.31*

YOVTH.

YOVTH. O Lorde, howe beastly they are, which are ledde by the sensualitie and pleasures of the fleshe.

1.Pet.2.12. AGE. It is very true my sonne : for so sayth Saint Peter, that those as bruite beastes, ledde with sensualitie, and made to be taken and destroyed, speake euill of those things whiche they knowe not, and shall perish through their owne corruption, and shall receyue the wages of vnrighteousnesse, as they which count it pleasure to liue deliciouslye for a season, spottes they are and blots, delyting themselues in their deceyuings and feastings.

YOVTH. What can be more plainly spoken and said against Dauncing, than is alreadye spoken and alledged by you ? I thanke God it hath done me much good, more than I am able to vtter.

AGE. What woulde these Fathers say nowe, if they were presently aliue, to see the wanton and filthie daunces that are nowe vsed in this cleare daye and light of the Gospell ? What Sabboth dayes, what other dayes are there, naye what nightes are ouerpassed without dauncing, among a number at this time? In Summer season howe doe the moste part of our yong men and maydes, in earely rising and getting themselues into the fieldes, at Dauncing, what foolishe toyes shall not a man see among them ? what vnchast countenances shall not be vsed then among them ? or what coales shall there be wanting that maye kindle Cupids desire? Truly none. Through this dauncing many maydens haue bene vnmaydened, whereby I may saye, it is the storehouse and nurserie of Bastardie. What adoe make our yong men at the time of May? Do they not vse nightwatchings to rob and steale yong trees out of other mens grounde, and bring them home into their Parishe, with minstrels playing before : & when they haue set it vp, they will decke it with floures and garlandes, Exod.32.6. 1.Cor.10.7. and daunce rounde (men and women togither, moste vnseemely and intollerable, as I haue proued before) about the tree, like vnto the children of Israell that daunced about the golden calfe that they had set vp. &c.

YOVTH. I maruayle much that the Magistrates doe suffer this

this to be vsed, especially where the Gospell is daily taught and preached.

A G E. It is greatly to be maruayled at in dede. But I may say as S. Paule sayd to the Romaines: These men which knew the lawe of God, howe that they which commit such things, are worthy of death, yet not onely do the same, but also fauour them that doe them. Which you know is as much as to consent to the, which is the full measure of all iniquitie, as the Prophete Esaye sayth: Thy rulers are rebellious, and companions of theeues. &c. Also you shall oftentimes see what graue women (yea suche as their either husbands are, or haue borne offices in a common weale) and others that make muche of their paynted sheathes, vse to daunce: It is for their recreation forsooth (say they) and then it is a worlde to see, nay a hell to see, howe they will swing, leape, & turne, when the Pypers and Crowders begin to play, as if they had neyther wisedome, grauitie, chastitie, sobrietie, honestie, or discretion, in such sort (doe they vse themselues in these wanton and vnchaste dauncings) that I cannot tell whether that Democritus hath more cause to laugh at their follies, than Heraclitus to weepe at their miseries. The Poet sayth:

Roma 1 ši.

Esay. 1.23.

> To dauncing come children, maydes, and wiues,
> And flattering yong men to seeke to haue their pray,
> The hand in hand great falshode oft contriues.
> The olde queane also this madnesse will assay,
> And the olde dotarde, though he scantly may
> For age and lamenesse stirre eyther foote or hande,
> Yet playeth he the foole with other in the bande.

Sebast. Frant. lib. Stultife-ranis.

What newe kinde of daunces, and newe deuised gestures the people haue deuised, and daylye doe deuise, it will grieue chaste eares to heare it, good eyes to see it, or tongue to vtter it: so that it may truly be verified that the wyse man sayth:

> He that will seeke for a dauncing place,
> Shall finde there all maners that lacketh grace.

C.iij.   YOVTH.

YOVTH. God graunt that we may leaue this filthie vyce of Dauncing among all the rest, and that the Magistrates and rulers may in such sort cut downe this wicked vice, that it may be no more vsed and exercised, and set sharpe punishment for the vsers and teachers thereof, as is most meete for them, so as God may be glorified and sinne abandoned.

AGE. You haue made a very good prayer, which I praye also vnto God it may take effect, for his mercies sake. Amen.

YOVTH. Nowe giue me to vnderstande, I praye you good father Age, what aunswere shall I make vnto them that will alledge and say, there must be some pleasures in our life and pastimes, whereby we may be recreated, and our wits refreshed, that are wearied with toyle, labour, and studie.

AGE. You must graunt them that: but in the meane time they must be admonished, that there are other pleasures more religious and honest, as Saint Paule sayth: Speake vnto your selues in psalmes and Hymnes, and spirituall songs, singing and making melodie to the Lorde in your heartes. Agayne he sayth: Let the worde of God dwell in you plenteously in all wisedome, teaching and admonishing your owne selues in Psalmes. &c. singing to the Lord with grace in your hearts. Also Saint James sayth: Is any among you afflicted? let him pray: Is any merie? let him sing. Saint Tertullian sayth, that Christians vsed assemblies togither, to their moderate shorte suppers, and when they were refreshed with meat, they sang diuine prayses, or recited some thing out of the holy Scriptures, prouoking one another by them, and by this meanes they returned home soberlye. So Syrach sayth: Stande vp betimes, and be not the last: but get thee home without delay, and there take thy pastime, and doe what thou wilt, so that thou doe no euill, or vse prowde wordes. But aboue al things, giue thanks vnto him that hath made thee, and replenished thee with his goodes. &c.

There are other honest pleasures, as Problemes, wherewith the wittes may be exercised and refreshed. There are notable histories, as the Actes and Monumentes of the Church, made by

that

Ephe.5.19.

Colos.3.16.

Iam.5.13.

Tertul.in Apologetico.

Eccl.32.12. 13,14.

that good and blessed manne maister John Fore. For hystories
(sayth Cicero) is a witnesse of tymes, the light of truth, the life
of memorie, the mystresse of lyfe, the messenger of antiquitie.&c. Those prayses certainlye are great, and yet they agree
not with euery kynde of hystories, but with those onely in which
these rules are obserued : namely, that it sette forth no lyes, or
bee afrayde to tell the truth, &c. Which in my conscience neuer
none wrote a more true and faythfull hystorie, then maister
John Fore hath (whatsoeuer the carping Papistes prate and
say to the contrarie) so that I say to you, there is no hystorie so
slender, which is not verye muche profitable for some parte of
mans life.

But aboue all, let them reade the holy Scriptures, and exercise themselues therein daye and night.&c. Saint Chrysostome
sayth : He that is ignorant shall finde to learne there : he that is
stubborne and a sinner, may finde there scourges : he that is troubled, may finde there ioyes and comfort of eternall life.&c. It is a
sea (sayth Gregorie) for Elephantes to swimme in, and the sillye
Lambe to walke in.&c. These are the exercises that we ought to
take our repast and pleasure in all the dayes of our lyfe.&c. Plato
sayth : That the life of a Philosopher is the meditation of death.
The like I may say, that the lyfe of a christian man is a perpetuall studie and exercise of mortifying the flesh, vntill it be vtterly slaine, the spirit getting the dominion in vs.

TOVTH. These are very good and godly exercises, and necessarie to bee vsed in these daungerous dayes wherein wee nowe
lyue.

AGE. In deede if they doe consider the daungerous times
that we are in, they haue litle cause to vse those follies, for in stead
of playing, they woulde vse praying : in steade of Dauncing, repenting : for ioye, sorowe : for laughing, mourning : for myrth,
sadnesse: for pride, patience: for wantonnesse, wofulnesse.&c. Is it
now (thinke you) a time to be mery, dice, daunce, and playe ? seeing before our eyes, howe the blouddie Papistes murther and
slaughter in all places rounde aboute vs oure poore brethren.

that

*Cic.lib.de
Oratore.*

*Psal.1.2.
Deut.6.6.
Iosua.1.8.
Prou.6.20.
Chrysost.in
Mat.22 ho.4
Grego ad
Leandrum.*

2.Kin.5.12.

Luc.19.41.

that professe the Gospell of Iesu Christ. Christ wept ouer Ierusalem for his eminent and imminent destruction, and doe we laugh at our brethrens destruction?

Luc.13.2.

Christ sayde to the Iewes: Suppose ye that those Galileans were greater sinners than all the other Galileans, bicause they haue suffered such things? I tell you nay: But excepte you amende your liues, ye shall all likewyse perishe. So I saye to thee Englande: Doest thou suppose that those French men, whiche

Exod.28.

were cruellye murthered, and vnnaturallye slaughtered by the bloudye and vnmercifull Papistes in Fraunce, were greater sinners than thou art? I tell thee nay: But excepte thou Englande amende thy manners, and bring forth better fruites of the Gospell, thou wilte likewise perishe also. For thou drawest ini-

Esay.5.18.
2.Peter.3.4
Eccl.4.17.

quitie with cordes of vanitie and sinne, as with Carte roapes. And yet as Salomon sayeth: They knowe not that they doe euill.

God graunt to open the eyes of Englande, that it maye see his sinnes, and be ashamed thereof, and fall to repentaunce, and

Ioel.1.13.15

to rent their heartes and not their garmentes, and turne to the Lorde God, for he is gracious and mercifull.&c. Lette the peo-

Ezech.18.

ple therfore be gathered togither, sanctifie the congregation, gather the Elders, assemble the children, and those that sucke the breastes: let the Bridegrome go forth of his chamber, and hys Bryde out of hir Bryde chamber, let the Priestes, the Ministers of the Lorde weepe betweene the Porche and the Altare, and let them saye: Spare thy people (O Lorde) and gyue not thyne heritage into reproche, that the Heathen Papistes shoulde

Mica.7.10.
Psal.42.10.

reygne ouer vs. Wherefore shoulde they say among the people: Where is their God?

YOVTH You haue made a godlye prayer, and the Lorde graunt it may take effecte in vs all: But I feare me it is, as it was in the tyme of Abraham: whyles hee prayed, the people

Ge.19.22.23.

played: whyles he wept, they laughed: whyles he desired, they deferred: and whyle hee persuaded God, they daylye prouoked God to anger.&c.

A GE.

A G E. Yet my sonne, Abraham left not to pray for them, neyther ought we, for no doubt but God hath his children, amõg the wicked of this world, as he had Lot among the Sodomits, Abdias with Achab and Iesabel, Nichodemus among the Pharises, Matthew and Zacheus among the toll takers, Paule among the persecuting lawyers and Scribes, &c.

1.Kings.19.18

Luke.19.1.

Y O V T H. Truely good father, I see that as they vsed Lot, so are the preachers now vsed, for the more they call them backe frõ playing and Dauncing, the faster they runne forwarde, the harder they crye, the deafer they are, the more they loue them, the worse they hate them.

Psal.58.4.5.
2.Cor.2.15.

A G E. That is lamentable, that the preachers are become their enimies for telling them truth, and their foes for helping them. The old saying is true, *Veritas odium parit:* Truth getteth hatred: yet they must not leaue off to preach the word continually, in season and out of season, improue, rebuke, exhort with all long sufferings and doctrine, let them cast out the seede of Gods word, and let the Lord alone with the increase therof.

Gala.4.16.

2.Timo.4.2.
Ezech.2.5.

1.Cor.3.7.

Y O V T H. There was neuer more preaching, & worse liuing, neuer more talking and lesse following, neuer more professing, and lesse profyting, neuer more wordes and fewer deedes, neuer trewer faith preached and lesse workes done, than is now, which is to be lamented and sorowed.

A G E. You must not nor ought not, to impute it vnto the preaching of Gods word, but vnto the wickednesse and peruerse nature of mans corruption: you know my sonne, by the buds and fruits of trees, times are discerned and known: So truely by these their fruites (which springeth of their corrupt and rotten trees of their flesh) we are taught in the Scriptures that the time of haruest is at hand.

Mat.24.32.
Luke.21.29.
Mar.16.2.3.
Mar 3.12.
Mat.24.57
Marke.13.32.
Luke 17.28.

For Christ sayth, that as the dayes of Noe were, so likewise shall the comming of the sonne of man be: for in the dayes before the flonde came, they did eate and drinke, mary, and gaue in mariage, plant, buy and sel &c. and knew nothing til the floud came and tooke them al away &c. he sayth also, iniquitie shal be increa-

Mat.24.12

Iohn 16.2.

sed, and the loue of many shall abate, the preachers shal be hated and euil spoken of, they shall bee excommunicated and killed, &c. And Paul also speaketh of those fruites (largely) that men shall bring forth in the last dayes, saying:

This knowe also, that in the latter dayes shal come perillous times, for men shal be louers of their owne selues, couetous, boasters, proude, cursed speakers, disobedient to parents, vnthankful, vnholy, without natural affection, trucebreakers, false accusers, intemperate, fierce, despisers of them which are good, traytours, heady, high minded, louers of pleasures more than louers of god, hauing a shewe of godlinesse &c. al which fruites wee may see euidently with our eyes, raigning too much in al estats & degrees. Therfore, it is no maruayle if they hate the light of Gods word: for that their deedes are so euill, and nowe made manifest to the world, for he y doth euil hateth y light, saith our sauiour Christ &c.

Iohn 3.19.

YOVTH. Truely you haue declared their fruites, wherby we may easily gather, that the day of iudgement is not far off, but al this while, they passe not for any exhortations, nor haue any regard and consideration in the day of iudgement: for they doe imagine with themselues, that there is no immortalitie of the soule, and that it is but a fable of Robyn hoode, to tel them of the day of iudgemente, and thinke death ought neuer to be remembred of them.

AGE: These are the same people, that saint Peter speaketh of, saying: This first vnderstand, that there shal come in the last dayes, mockers, which wil walke after their lusts, and say, where is the promise of his comming? for since the fathers died, all things continue alike from the beginning of the creation. Euen such as those Epicures, and Atheistes which you speake of. And Syrach sheweth the reason, why these wicked ones cannot abide, death. O saith he, how bitter is the remembrance of death to a mã that liueth at rest in his possessions and pleasures &c. Althoughe they vse to say (for a little time) come let vs inioy the pleasures y are present, let vs al be partakers of our wantonnesse: let vs leaue some token of our pleasure in euery place: For that is our portion and

2.Pet.3.3.4

Eccle.4.1.

and this is our Lot, but one day they shal cry out and say, in bitternesse of conscience(if they repent not in time) what hath pride prospered vs? or what profit hath the pompe of riches and pleasures brought vs?al these things are passed away like a shadow, and as a post that passeth by. Therfore sayth Salomon, the hope of the vngodly is like the dust ȳ is blowen away with the winde, and like a thinne fome that is scattered abroad with the storme, and as the smoke that is dispersed with the winde, and as the remembraunce of him passeth, that tarieth but for a day: but the righteous shal liue for euer:their reward also is with the Lord, & the most high hath care of them, &c.

VVis.2.6.7.8.9.
VVisdom.5.8.9.
1.Chro.2ȳ.15.

Cap.25.

Now my sonne Youth, time calleth me away, I wil take my leaue and commit you to the tuitiō of the Almightie:for I must hasten homeward:and loke what I haue sayde to you, kepe it, & practise it all your life long,loke backe no more to filthy Sodom, least it happen to you as did to Lots wife, neither turne to your vomet like a dogge, neyther yet to your filthy puddle and myre, like a swyne,for if you do,your portiō wil be with those that shal be shut out of gods kingdome.For if you,after you haue escaped from the filthinesse of the worlde, through the knowledge of the Lord, are yet intãgled again therin,and ouercome,the latter end is worse with you than the beginning.&c. Therfore be neuer obliuious,for as the wiseman saith:

Eccle.6.36.

Tantum scimus quantum memoria tenemus.

So much we know assuredly,
As we do hold in memory.

YOVTH. I giue you most humble thankes,for your good and godly counsel and fatherly instructiōs:and by gods grace I shall hereafter hate(among al other vices)this naughty loytering idlenesse:prodigal & wastful Diceplaying,and filthy wanton Dauncing,& I wil draw and perswade as many as I can or may (by any meanes)frō it likewise, & by the grace of Iesus Christ,I shal neuer let slip out of my minde, these your godly sayings and fatherly instructions,but wil write them vp in my hart.

Eccle.6.36.37.

Psal.51.13
Luke.22.32.
Eccle.6.56.

T.ij.   AGE.

AGE. If you so do, it is very wel: and in al your actions and doings, what soeuer you take in hande, remember the ende, and you shal neuer do amisse.

YOVTH. God graunt that I may so do.

AGE. Farewel my son Youth, God blesse thee, and rule thee alwayes with his holy spirit in the end and to the end.

YOVTH. And you also good father, for his Christes sake. Amen.

FINIS.

IMPRINTED AT LONdon by Henry Bynneman for George Bishop.